BOBBY GALLAGHER

Hopelessly Devoted

The Ultimate Unofficial Fan Guide to Olivia Newton-John

Copyright © 2025 by Bobby Gallagher

All rights reserved. No part of this publication may be reproduced, stored or transmitted in any form or by any means, electronic, mechanical, photocopying, recording, scanning, or otherwise without written permission from the publisher. It is illegal to copy this book, post it to a website, or distribute it by any other means without permission.

Bobby Gallagher asserts the moral right to be identified as the author of this work.

Bobby Gallagher has no responsibility for the persistence or accuracy of URLs for external or third-party Internet Websites referred to in this publication and does not guarantee that any content on such Websites is, or will remain, accurate or appropriate.

Designations used by companies to distinguish their products are often claimed as trademarks. All brand names and product names used in this book and on its cover are trade names, service marks, trademarks and registered trademarks of their respective owners. The publishers and the book are not associated with any product or vendor mentioned in this book. None of the companies referenced within the book have endorsed the book.

First edition

This book was professionally typeset on Reedsy. Find out more at reedsy.com

Contents

1	Introduction	1
2	If Not for You	6
3	Let Me Be There	10
4	You're the One That I Want	15
5	Let's Get Physical	19
6	Magic	23
7	Stronger Than Before	27
8	Grace and Gratitude	31
9	A Little More Love	35
10	Heartstrings and Halos	39
11	I Honestly Love You	44
12	Don't Stop Believin'	48
13	Twist of Fate	52
14	Soul Kiss	56
15	The Right Moment	60
16	Gaia	64
17	A Little More Love	68
18	Magic	72
19	Warm and Tender	76
20	Carry Me Home	80
21	Hopelessly Devoted	84
22	Author's Note: Thank You for Devoting With Me	88
23	Discography: Olivia Newton-John	90

24 Fan Fun 93

1

Introduction

"**I honestly love you.**" - **Olivia Newton-John**

Some voices don't just echo - they *glow*. They don't shout for attention or chase trends. They simply arrive, gentle and luminous, and before you know it, they've taken up permanent residence in your heart. Olivia Newton-John had one of those voices. The kind that felt like a hug in the dark. The kind that could make you believe in love again, even on your lowest day. The kind that didn't just fill the room - it *lifted* it.

I was probably too young to remember the first time I *heard* Olivia, but I *felt* her long before I knew who she was. Maybe it was "Magic" drifting through a supermarket speaker, or "Have You Never Been Mellow" lulling through the radio on some lazy Sunday drive. But then came *Grease*. The hair. The hips. The high notes. And suddenly, Olivia Newton-John wasn't just a voice - she was a cultural force.

This book isn't a dusty, buttoned-up biography. This is a love letter. A mixtape. A late-night tribute written by the light of a lava lamp. It's *Hopelessly Devoted*, because how else could we describe what Olivia inspired in fans across the decades? This is for the teens who dreamed of being Sandy, the disco dancers who lived for "Physical," the country lovers who clung to every word of "Please Mr. Please," and the believers who followed her beyond music - into healing, hope, and quiet heroism.

Because Olivia Newton-John wasn't just a singer. Or a movie star. Or a cancer warrior. Or a wellness pioneer. She was all of it - and then some. A woman of contradictions who made them all harmonize. She could be soft and fierce, ethereal and grounded, glamorous and goofy. She could reinvent herself a dozen times and somehow still feel like the same girl who once crooned, "If not for you…"

✧ *From Sweetheart to Superstar*

Born in England, raised in Australia, and launched into orbit somewhere in Nashville before landing squarely in the Hollywood hills, Olivia's career is the stuff of musical legend. She began in the country-pop crossover lane and swerved - stylishly - into mainstream superstardom. She had charm, yes, but she had *chops*. A four-time Grammy winner. Over 100 million records sold. A sound that could flirt with folk, slide into disco, dance through soft rock, and land, effortlessly, in the hearts of millions.

And then came *Grease*. Let's just say the world was never the same again.

Sandy Olsson – sweet, nervy, fresh-faced Sandy – was already iconic by the time she slid into those black leather pants. But Olivia *owned* her. She didn't just act; she transcended. That final walk down the fairground strip in "You're the One That I Want" didn't just transform Sandy. It transformed *pop culture.* And it gave us one of the most watched, rewatched, karaoke-bellowed duets in history. (Let's face it – we've *all* tried to hit that "You better shape up!" at some point, and none of us quite nailed it like Olivia.)

💚 *Beyond the Spotlight*

But Olivia didn't stop at fame. She pivoted. Reinvented. Stripped it all back. She became an advocate before it was trendy, a wellness guru before there were hashtags. Diagnosed with breast cancer in the early 1990s, she chose transparency and courage, becoming a beacon for millions navigating illness and fear. She didn't disappear into pain – she transformed it into purpose. Her work with the Olivia Newton-John Cancer Wellness & Research Centre in Melbourne is just one of the many legacies she leaves behind that have *nothing* to do with gold records or Top 10 hits.

And yet, even as she evolved into an activist, a businesswoman, and a symbol of quiet strength, Olivia never stopped *singing.* Her voice remained – crystalline, calming, utterly unmistakable. It was a voice that aged like vintage wine – mellow, wise, and more soulful with every passing year.

Even in her later recordings – duets, charity singles, holiday albums – there was that signature warmth. A voice that didn't need to belt to make you feel. A voice that *invited* you in, gently, with grace.

✨ *What This Book Is (and Isn't)*

This book isn't here to tell you everything Olivia Newton-John ever did. You can find that on Wikipedia. This is a *fan guide* - but not in the twee, shallow way that sometimes sounds. This is *ultimate. Unofficial.* And *devoted.* It's a deep dive into the moments that made her magic, the lyrics that lingered, the interviews that showed her sparkle, and the reinventions that kept her ever relevant.

You'll find:

- Chapters that trace her genre-hopping brilliance, from Nashville to neon.
- Stories behind the scenes of *Grease, Xanadu,* and the albums that shaped a generation.
- Spotlights on her activism, her holistic philosophy, and her courage in the face of cancer.
- And most of all, you'll find a steady through-line of love - for her fans, her art, and the world she tried so hard to heal.

We'll dance through the highs, cry through the lows, and skate (yes, literally - just wait for the *Xanadu* chapter) through every transformation that made Olivia Newton-John not just a star, but a *light.*

INTRODUCTION

So pour yourself a glass of something fizzy. Press play on your favorite ONJ playlist. And get ready to revisit the legacy of a woman who showed us that being soft was never a weakness – it was her greatest strength. She didn't just ask the world to love her – she made us want to.

This one's for the dreamers. The rollerskaters. The karaoke queens. The quiet warriors. And every hopelessly devoted heart who ever believed that music could heal – because Olivia Newton-John proved that it absolutely could.

Let's begin.

Bobby

2

If Not for You

"*If not for you, my sky would fall / Rain would gather too...*"

Every voice has a beginning. Some explode onto the scene in a burst of noise and neon, demanding to be heard. Others arrive gently, like morning light through a kitchen window - soft, steady, impossible to ignore. Olivia Newton-John had the latter. Hers was a voice that didn't scream to be noticed. It *glowed*. It invited. And before the world knew it, that quiet glow would light up stages across continents.

She was born on September 26, 1948, in Cambridge, England - a city of cloisters and classical minds - into a family that read more like a Who's Who of intellectual brilliance. Her father, Brinley Newton-John, was a man of order and intellect, a former MI5 officer during the war who helped with the decoding of Nazi messages at Bletchley Park. Her mother, Irene, was the daughter of Max Born, a Nobel Prize–winning physicist and close associate of Albert Einstein. In any other family, this might have been the expected trajectory - academia, science, the pursuit of measurable truth. But Olivia? She followed something else entirely: the pull of melody, emotion, and unspoken connection.

When Olivia was six, the Newton-John family emigrated to Australia, landing in the golden sprawl of Melbourne. It was a move that shifted everything – landscape, culture, energy. Gone were the grey English skies; in their place came the vast warmth of the Australian sun, the freedom of space, the casual possibility that anything might happen. And for a girl who'd always been quietly humming under her breath, it felt like the kind of place where a voice could grow wings.

Music came naturally. Not with drama or performance, but with a kind of shy sincerity that would become her trademark. By the age of 14, Olivia had already begun forming schoolgirl groups with sweetly clumsy names like Sol Four and performing at the local coffee houses. There was a nervousness in her stage presence, but the kind that made you lean in – a kind of raw, unpolished charm that didn't try to dazzle, just *connect*. Even then, people noticed the tone. That voice. Not just technically lovely – although it was – but emotionally tuned in, always just on the right side of tender.

Her first major break came when she entered and won a local television talent competition called *Sing, Sing, Sing*. The prize? A trip to London. For most teenagers, that might have felt like fantasy. But for Olivia, it was a beginning. She boarded that plane with the weightlessness of someone not yet aware of her own destiny. She was just following the music, wherever it might lead.

London in the late 1960s was everything – a whirlwind of sound, style, reinvention. And Olivia, ever the chameleon, stepped into it with quiet purpose. She partnered with her close friend Pat Carroll, forming the singing duo "Pat and Olivia," performing in cabarets and nightclubs, bouncing around the edges of the British pop scene. They wore matching dresses, sang sweet harmonies, and charmed everyone from local producers to crusty club owners. But even then, Olivia was the standout - not because she demanded it, but because she couldn't help it. Her voice had that unteachable quality: the ability to sound like it was singing *just to you.*

When Carroll returned to Australia, Olivia stayed. She knew there was something to chase - something she hadn't quite named yet, but that she could feel in her bones. She cut singles that mostly went unnoticed, took minor roles in low-budget musical films, and made frequent appearances on the UK television circuit. It wasn't glamorous work, but it was *steady.* It was the grind behind every future icon, the string of almosts before the first real *yes.*

That first yes came quietly - a song recorded in 1971, a cover of Bob Dylan's "If Not for You." Dylan had written it in that raw, gruff style only he could, and George Harrison had already covered it with his signature slide guitar smoothness. But Olivia? She did something different. She made it *breathe.* Her version was fresh-faced and honest, shimmering with that signature clarity that would soon become her calling card. It wasn't edgy or cool or rebellious. But it was *true.* And that truth caught ears.

The single charted. Modestly, but meaningfully. Enough to open doors. Enough to suggest that maybe this girl with the feather-blonde hair and the impossibly kind eyes wasn't just another singer passing through. She had staying power - and she was just getting started.

Her debut album, also titled *If Not for You*, followed later that year, blending country, pop, and soft rock into a sonic palette that felt distinctly Olivia. It wasn't chasing trends - it was crafting something quieter, gentler, more melodic than the brash sounds of the early '70s charts. And it worked. Slowly, steadily, the world began to lean in.

Looking back, that first hit feels almost poetic in its choice. *If Not for You.* Because in many ways, that's what the world would end up whispering back to Olivia, again and again. If not for you - who else would've shown us how to be soft and strong at once? If not for you - who else would've made vulnerability feel like a superpower? If not for you - how else would we have made it through those breakups, those heartaches, those longing-filled nights?

From the cobbled streets of Cambridge to the sunny sprawls of Melbourne, from café stages to Top of the Pops, Olivia Newton-John was never loud, never brash, never in your face. But her presence was undeniable. She was the kind of artist who didn't announce herself - she just arrived, like spring after a long winter, and made everything bloom.

3

Let Me Be There

"*Let me be there in your morning / Let me be there in your night...*"

By the early 1970s, Olivia Newton-John had done something quietly radical - she'd slipped into the international music scene without the noise or bravado of many of her contemporaries. While the rock gods of the day were shredding guitars and lighting up stadiums, Olivia was carving a gentler path. Her music didn't shake the ground - it warmed it. She wasn't chasing rebellion. She was offering refuge.

After the success of *If Not for You*, Olivia doubled down on what she did best - that delicate blend of country-pop warmth and girl-next-door sincerity. Her voice, honeyed and heartbreak-ready, found its natural home in a style that was equal parts Nashville and Notting Hill. It was a curious mix at first - a British-Australian singer channeling the Tennessee sound - but somehow, it worked. It *really* worked.

Her 1973 album *Let Me Be There* marked a turning point. The title track was pure earworm - breezy, catchy, and comforting all at once. But more than that, it gave Olivia something she hadn't fully held yet: American recognition. The song didn't just chart - it crossed borders. In the U.S., it climbed into the Top Ten and refused to budge. Country stations embraced her. Pop radio welcomed her. And fans? They fell, hard.

The brilliance of Olivia's approach during this time wasn't in pushing boundaries - it was in *blurring* them. Her music gently dissolved the walls between country and pop, between tradition and trend. There was a reason the Nashville crowd took to her with such affection. Despite her accent, despite her non-American roots, Olivia sang country with the kind of authenticity you can't fake. There was no twang-for-hire, no novelty angle. Just emotion. Earnestness. A woman singing stories with her whole heart.

And Nashville responded. Big time.

In 1974, Olivia Newton-John did what many thought impossible: she won the Grammy Award for Best Female Country Vocal Performance for "Let Me Be There." It was a seismic moment - not just for Olivia, but for the genre itself. Country purists didn't quite know what to do with her. She wasn't Loretta or Dolly. She wasn't sipping whiskey or riding tractors. She was Olivia - a fresh-faced, soft-voiced songbird who sang about devotion and longing without needing to shout. And somehow, that quietness felt like a revolution.

The accolades poured in. A CMA award. A wave of television appearances. Sold-out shows in cities she'd barely had time to learn how to pronounce. America, it seemed, was catching on to something that fans in Australia and the UK already knew:

Olivia Newton-John was the real deal.

And yet, through all the glitter and gold, Olivia stayed remarkably grounded. There was never a sense of image-manufacturing or tabloid manipulation. She smiled like someone who still couldn't quite believe this was all happening. In interviews, she was gracious, humble, sometimes even self-deprecating. Fame didn't seem to change her - it just gave her a bigger microphone.

Her next few albums built on that momentum. *Long Live Love* (1974), *If You Love Me, Let Me Know* (also 1974), and *Have You Never Been Mellow* (1975) didn't just keep her on the charts - they *owned* them. The latter would become her first U.S. No. 1 album, cementing her place as a bona fide pop-country princess. The title track, "Have You Never Been Mellow," was a soft-spoken anthem for the weary. In an age of protest songs and disco fever, Olivia offered a reminder to breathe. To slow down. To feel.

It's easy to underestimate the power of that - especially now, in retrospect. But Olivia's music during these years wasn't just pleasant background noise. It was *emotional architecture*. It shaped the atmosphere of countless living rooms, car rides, and teenage daydreams. She gave permission to be gentle in a loud, fast world. And that mattered. It still does.

And let's not forget the fashion. The early '70s Olivia look was all flowing dresses, soft curls, and sunshine smiles. There was something undeniably wholesome about her image - not calculated, just *natural*. She looked like someone you could trust. Someone you'd want to sing you to sleep. In a world of glam and grit, Olivia was the calm in the storm.

But beneath that softness was a steely kind of ambition. Not aggressive. Not cutthroat. But focused. Olivia wasn't just wandering through the industry waiting for hits to fall into her lap. She was paying attention - to her sound, her team, her audience. She knew who she was, even if the world was still figuring it out.

Behind the scenes, she began to take more control of her recordings. She didn't write many of her early hits, but she chose them carefully. She was drawn to songs that carried a certain emotional weight - songs that *meant* something. And when she sang them, they took on a life beyond the lyrics. You believed her. You felt seen.

By 1976, Olivia had not only conquered the pop-country charts - she'd become one of the most recognizable and beloved artists of the decade. Her name was synonymous with warmth, femininity, and effortless class. She wasn't controversial. She wasn't polarizing. She was *loved*. Unreservedly.

But even as she basked in the glow of radio dominance and Grammy glory, something else was stirring - a sense that she was ready for more. Something bigger. A reinvention, perhaps. A leap into another world entirely.

Because Olivia Newton-John, for all her gentleness, was never static. She moved like water - graceful, adaptable, and always forward. And on the horizon, something sparkled. Something cinematic. Something with a leather jacket and a T-Bird.

But before Grease would change everything, Olivia had already proved one very important thing: she didn't need a movie to make her a star.

She already was one.

4

You're the One That I Want

"*You better shape up, 'cause I need a man / And my heart is set on you...*"

Sometimes, a single role doesn't just change a career - it changes a life. It shifts public perception, resets the cultural clock, and places a pin on the map of pop history. For Olivia Newton-John, that role was Sandy Olsson in *Grease*. It wasn't just a character. It was a transformation. A reveal. A glittering moment where Olivia didn't just sing the song - she *became* it.

By the late 1970s, Olivia was already a chart-topping sensation, her albums weaving gentle paths through pop and country, her name synonymous with warmth, femininity, and a soft-spoken kind of fame. But Hollywood was a different beast. A hit record didn't guarantee a hit role, and many wondered if Olivia - the wholesome Aussie singer with the girl-next-door smile - could really carry a movie, especially one soaked in Americana, attitude, and adolescent angst.

But then John Travolta called.

Fresh off the wild success of *Saturday Night Fever*, Travolta had been cast as greaser heartthrob Danny Zuko in a big-screen adaptation of the hit Broadway musical *Grease*. And when the producers asked who he thought should play Sandy, Travolta didn't hesitate - he wanted Olivia. He'd seen her sing, watched her presence fill a room, and sensed there was something magic simmering just below the surface. Something the world hadn't quite seen yet.

Still, Olivia was hesitant. She was in her late twenties playing a teenager, she'd had a less-than-stellar experience in a previous film (*Toomorrow*, anyone?), and she wasn't sure if stepping into Hollywood would be a leap forward or a costly misstep. But then she met Travolta in person. And everything changed.

Their chemistry was instant - effortless, charming, quietly electric. Travolta was all swagger and softness. Olivia was composed but curious. Together, they clicked in that intangible way certain screen pairs just do. It wasn't scripted - it *sparked*. And Olivia, sensing something special, agreed to take the role... but with one condition. She wanted a screen test.

She needed to know - *really* know - that she could do this. That she could be Sandy. That she wouldn't just be a singer playing a part, but someone who belonged on that screen, in that story, at that moment. The screen test confirmed everything. Olivia had *it*. Whatever *it* was, she had it in spades.

Filming began in 1977, and from the very start, Olivia's presence on set radiated that blend of humility and magnetism that had always defined her. While the rest of the cast leaned into the larger-than-life energy of the musical, Olivia played Sandy with sincerity. She wasn't trying to steal scenes - she was just being present. Real. Honest. And that's exactly why she stole every scene anyway.

Sandy Olsson, in Olivia's hands, became something deeper than a stock character. She wasn't just a shy girl with good manners and a poodle skirt – she was vulnerable, hopeful, quietly fierce. Olivia brought layers to Sandy that could've easily been overlooked: the ache of trying to fit in, the sting of teenage insecurity, the slow-burning courage to claim her space. And when that transformation moment came – the tight black trousers, the tousled curls, the smoky eye and the strut that rewrote every rule – it wasn't just a costume change. It was a declaration.

That scene – that final walk down the funfair, cigarette in hand, hips swinging to the beat of "You're the One That I Want" – didn't just redefine Sandy. It redefined *Olivia*. The world had known her as the gentle balladeer, the breathy soprano with a halo of golden hair. But now? She was electric. Empowered. Unstoppable. Olivia wasn't playing at being bold – she *was* bold. And the audience felt it in their bones.

The soundtrack exploded. "You're the One That I Want" shot straight to number one in the U.S., the UK, Australia – everywhere. "Hopelessly Devoted to You," Olivia's aching solo ballad written specifically for the film, earned her an Academy Award nomination and became one of the most beloved torch songs of all time. And "Summer Nights"? Let's just say, if you've ever been near a karaoke machine, you already know the lyrics by heart.

Grease wasn't just a film. It was a movement. It became the highest-grossing musical of its time, a cultural juggernaut that launched fashion trends, dance routines, and fan obsessions that still ripple today. But at the heart of it all was Olivia – gentle yet commanding, radiant yet grounded. She anchored the film with emotion and grace, reminding us that strength doesn't always shout. Sometimes it sings in perfect pitch.

In interviews, Olivia later reflected on how transformative the role had been. Not just professionally - though it undeniably launched her into a new stratosphere of fame - but personally. Sandy had unlocked something in her. A confidence. A playfulness. A new way of being seen. And after years of being gently typecast as the sweetheart, Olivia now had the freedom to explore edgier, more modern territory. She had broken out of the mold - and it had glittered as it shattered.

The success of *Grease* rippled into every corner of her career. Her next moves would lean further into pop, into fashion, into reinvention. But this was the hinge point. The moment when Olivia Newton-John stopped being just a star - and became a legend.

And perhaps what makes that moment so unforgettable is that it wasn't forced. Olivia didn't reinvent herself to chase relevance. She simply *expanded*. She let the world see more of her - the fun, the fire, the flirtation - and the world responded with open arms.

For every young girl who ever felt too quiet, too sweet, too unsure - Sandy's transformation was a revelation. Not because she changed for a man, as the critics liked to say, but because she claimed her *own* power. And that message, sung through Olivia's voice, still echoes like the final chord of a perfect song.

5

Let's Get Physical

"*There's nothing left to talk about unless it's horizontally...*"
When Olivia Newton-John released *Physical* in 1981, it was as if she'd stepped through a time warp and landed not just in a new decade, but in a whole new dimension of herself. The softness of the seventies was gone - not abandoned, but evolved. In its place stood a woman unafraid to flirt, to flex, and to reframe her image with a cheeky wink and a pop beat. Gone were the flowing dresses and wistful ballads. In their place: neon, synths, sweatbands, and the most sexually suggestive No. 1 single of the decade.

And yet, Olivia pulled it off with all the charm and charisma that had made her a household name - because underneath the spandex and sultry lyrics, the same Olivia was still there. The warmth, the poise, the unmistakable voice. It had simply found a new beat.

The story of *Physical* begins with a song that was almost too risky for its time. Written by Steve Kipner and Terry Shaddick, "Physical" was originally offered to Rod Stewart and then to Tina Turner. Both passed. It was catchy, sure, but also brazen -

daring, even. The lyrics left little to the imagination. And Olivia? She almost passed too.

She wasn't quite sure it fit. The song was bold, almost confrontational in its innuendo. For someone whose image had long leaned toward sweet and sincere, this was unfamiliar territory. But Olivia wasn't the same woman who had once shied away from *Grease*. She had grown - not just in fame, but in confidence. She recorded it. And the moment she heard it back, she knew: this was going to be huge.

It wasn't just a hit. It was a *phenomenon*. "Physical" shot to No. 1 on the Billboard Hot 100 and stayed there for ten consecutive weeks, making it the longest-running chart-topper of 1981. The track was irrepressible - bouncy, bold, a perfect storm of early '80s production and Olivia's pristine vocals. And the music video? That pastel-hued, gym-set fever dream of toned bodies and aerobic antics? Instant classic. It played nonstop on MTV in its infancy, turning Olivia into one of the first true video-era icons.

But as with so much of Olivia's career, the brilliance wasn't just in the aesthetic. It was in the *balance*. She took a song laced with double entendres and sang it with a kind of playful, raised-eyebrow innocence. It was sexy, yes - but not aggressive. Bold, but not brash. She managed to flirt with taboo and keep her dignity firmly intact. It was pop performance as tightrope walk, and Olivia never missed a step.

The *Physical* album followed and proved there was more than one spark in this reinvention. Tracks like "Make a Move on Me" and "Landslide" showed off her growing confidence as a full-fledged pop star, capable of navigating the synth-pop landscape without losing the emotional clarity that had defined her ballads. This was Olivia stepping fully into the '80s, shoulder pads and all, and doing it on *her* terms.

She took the momentum on the road, launching her *Physical Tour* with dazzling lights, choreography, and a sense of theatricality she'd never fully embraced before. It was a show - in every sense of the word - and it allowed Olivia to explore the persona she'd only hinted at during her *Grease* days. Audiences lapped it up. Critics praised her. And a generation of fans who'd grown up with Sandy Olsson were now lining up to sweat it out with Olivia 2.0.

But as always, reinvention wasn't just about costumes and chord changes. It was about growth. And behind the scenes, Olivia was quietly becoming a powerhouse - a woman taking control of her image, her sound, and her direction. She wasn't simply playing dress-up in a new decade's wardrobe. She was steering the ship.

She began producing more of her own material, shaping her sound with precision. She worked closely with video directors, choreographers, and stylists to ensure her vision was realized down to the last blush-pink dumbbell. And all of it - the sultry lyrics, the eye-catching visuals, the chart-smashing singles - came from a place of genuine artistic exploration. Olivia wasn't just chasing hits. She was following her curiosity, her instincts, her evolution.

The backlash, of course, came as it always does when women dare to take control of their image. Some critics clutched their pearls, questioning the "appropriateness" of the song. A few country radio stations dropped her, claiming she'd strayed too far from the sweet sound that had made her famous. But Olivia didn't flinch. She understood the game - and more importantly, she was rewriting the rules.

If anything, the reaction only confirmed how powerful her pivot truly was. "Physical" wasn't just a song. It was a statement. About ownership. About self-expression. About shaking off the limitations of other people's expectations. Olivia had spent the '70s being beloved for her purity - and now she was showing that women can be multi-faceted. They can be gentle *and* bold. Innocent *and* provocative. Devoted *and* empowered.

Even now, decades later, "Physical" pulses with that same infectious confidence. It's in workout playlists, wedding receptions, and the background of more '80s flashback scenes than we can count. But for those who were there - who remember that moment when Olivia stepped into the gym in that iconic headband and winked at the camera - it was more than just a bop. It was a cultural reset.

And Olivia? She never once looked like she wasn't having the time of her life.

6

Magic

"*You have to believe we are magic / Nothin' can stand in our way...*"

It takes a certain kind of star to walk into a glowing roller-disco fantasy, play a Greek muse come to life, and somehow make it all feel completely natural. But then again, Olivia Newton-John was never your average star. She didn't just shine - she radiated something softer, stranger, and more enchanting. And in *Xanadu*, she stepped into a world as whimsical and otherworldly as the voice that carried her there.

By 1980, Olivia had conquered both the music charts and the silver screen. *Grease* had made her a cinematic sensation. *Physical* was just around the corner, poised to electrify the pop world. But in between those two defining moments came a film so gleefully bizarre, so drenched in glitter and glowing with neon, that it transcended mere flop status to become something else entirely: a cult classic. A fever dream. A roller-skating, genre-bending monument to the weird and the wonderful.

Xanadu was, on paper, a gamble. Part musical, part fantasy, part love letter to the 1940s and the 1980s in equal measure, it followed a struggling artist (played by Michael Beck) who meets a mysterious muse named Kira - played, of course, by Olivia - who inspires him to open a roller disco. That's right. A *roller disco*. With glowing wheels, Grecian gowns, and Gene Kelly doing his final on-screen dance number. And somehow, it *worked*. Or rather, it didn't - not in the way studios wanted. Critics panned it. Audiences scratched their heads. But for a certain kind of dreamer, it was exactly the kind of magical mess we never stopped loving.

And Olivia? She was luminous. Whether gliding across the screen in flowing chiffon or beaming from behind those iconic skates, she embodied the kind of ethereal optimism that *Xanadu* needed to hold itself together. Kira wasn't just a muse in the script - Olivia *was* the muse, infusing the whole film with a kind of grounded sparkle. Without her, the whole thing might have fallen apart. But with her? It became unforgettable.

Where the film faltered, the music soared. The *Xanadu* soundtrack is still, to this day, one of the most joyfully eclectic albums of the 1980s. Olivia teamed up with the Electric Light Orchestra - Jeff Lynne's symphonic rock vision crashing headfirst into Olivia's pure pop sensibility - and what emerged was pure alchemy. Tracks like "Magic," "Suddenly," and the title song "Xanadu" weren't just good. They were *fantastic*. The kind of songs that make your heart lift without asking permission.

"Magic," in particular, became one of Olivia's most enduring hits. A slow-burning, synth-laced anthem of hope and belief, it wrapped its arms around listeners in the same way Olivia's best work always did. It reached No. 1 on the Billboard Hot 100 and stayed there for four weeks – proof that even when the film confused critics, the *soundtrack* moved the people. And really, that's always been the Newton-John way. Even when the world tried to put her in a box, she floated just outside of it, powered by melody, emotion, and a little bit of moonlight.

Xanadu, as a film, may never have gotten the red-carpet respect it hoped for, but it became something rarer: a shared secret among fans. The kind of film you quote, sing, and giggle about with people who *get it*. It lives in drag shows and roller rinks, in midnight screenings and glitter-drenched playlists. And Olivia? She embraced it. She never rolled her eyes at it. Never distanced herself from it. She understood that sometimes art isn't about critical consensus. Sometimes it's about joy.

Behind the scenes, *Xanadu* also marked a shift in Olivia's own creative confidence. She was more involved in the musical direction, shaping her sound alongside producers who understood where she wanted to go. There was less country, more cosmic. Less soft twang, more sweeping synthesizers. This was Olivia leaning into the future, not with calculated cool, but with wide-eyed willingness.

The visuals from *Xanadu* – the rainbow-hued gowns, the galaxy-lit dance floors, the surreal sequences that blurred stage and dream – became part of her evolving image. It was theatrical, yes, but never fake. She brought sincerity to even the most surreal scenes. When Olivia skated in slow motion, smiling beneath a halo of curls, you *believed* in magic. You believed in her.

It's worth noting, too, how gracefully she carried the aftermath.

When the reviews came in - brutal, even mocking - Olivia didn't spiral. She didn't retreat. She kept moving, kept recording, kept reinventing. That resilience, that refusal to let public perception define her path, is part of what made her so beloved. She never let cynicism in. Not really. She kept singing. Kept smiling. Kept skating toward something brighter.

Years later, *Xanadu* would be adapted into a Broadway musical - a tongue-in-cheek tribute that leaned into the camp and chaos of the original with affection, not apology. And Olivia? She cheered it on, laughing along with the audience, as always in on the joke, but never the butt of it.

That's the real legacy of *Xanadu*. Not just a misunderstood film, but a moment in time when Olivia Newton-John showed us that it's okay to go big. To be a little silly. To chase beauty even when it doesn't quite make sense. And to do it all with grace, even when the world doesn't know what to make of you.

Because sometimes, being timeless isn't about perfection.

It's about believing in magic - and never skating away from it.

7

Stronger Than Before

"*I've been in darkness / I've been in light / I'm just surviving, but I'm still alive...*"

The first time Olivia Newton-John heard the word "cancer" directed at her, it didn't arrive with any poetic gravity. It wasn't cinematic. It was clinical. Matter-of-fact. Breast cancer. A diagnosis she received in 1992, on the same weekend her beloved father passed away. It was the kind of double blow that could fold a person in half - grief and fear colliding in one brutal, breathless moment.

But Olivia didn't collapse. She *stepped forward*. Quietly. Bravely. Without fanfare. And in doing so, she began a new chapter - not of music or movies, but of meaning. A chapter that revealed just how strong, generous, and utterly radiant she truly was.

Up until then, Olivia's career had been about connection. Whether she was singing about love, heartbreak, or disco-fuelled desire, she did so with a sincerity that made fans feel understood. But her personal journey through illness added a new layer to that connection. It wasn't staged. It wasn't stylised. It was real. And she chose to share it - not as a celebrity, but as a woman navigating a path that far too many others knew all too well.

She underwent surgery and chemotherapy, keeping her circle close, her heart open, and her public statements measured. There was no drama in her disclosures. No tabloid confessions. Just honesty. Clarity. She spoke about her experience in a way that made others feel less alone, using her platform to shine a light on early detection, self-exams, and the emotional toll of cancer that doesn't always show up in scans.

But Olivia didn't stop at awareness. She wanted to *build* something. To leave a legacy not just in vinyl and film reels, but in bricks and mortar. And so, in 2008, the doors opened on the Olivia Newton-John Cancer Wellness & Research Centre in Melbourne - a world-class facility offering both cutting-edge treatment and holistic care. It wasn't just a hospital. It was a healing space. A place where patients could find not just medicine, but music, massage, meditation - a little hope wrapped in compassion.

Olivia poured herself into the project. Fundraising, speaking, showing up. She wasn't just a name on the door. She was in the room, holding hands, listening to stories, offering her own. Her advocacy wasn't performative. It was persistent. Personal. Purposeful.

And through it all, she kept creating.

Her music during these years reflected that evolution. Albums like *Gaia: One Woman's Journey* felt like sonic diaries - intimate, spiritual, deeply human. Gone were the chart-chasing pop tracks. In their place were songs about resilience, connection, and inner strength. "Stronger Than Before," "Don't Cut Me Down," and "Not Gonna Give Into It" weren't just lyrics – they were lifelines. Not just for Olivia, but for anyone who had ever stared down fear and chosen to sing anyway.

She embraced alternative medicine as a companion to her treatment – acupuncture, plant-based diets, herbal supplements – and spoke openly about finding balance between science and spirit. She wasn't prescriptive. She didn't preach. She simply shared what helped her heal, and let others find their own path in that light.

And she kept showing up. For concerts. For causes. For survivors. Her *Liv Aid* breast self-exam device helped educate women around the world. Her annual wellness walks raised millions. And every time she stepped on stage in those years – whether in an intimate benefit or a global broadcast – there was a quiet kind of triumph in her smile. Not just because she'd survived. But because she was *living*.

Olivia's approach to illness was never about denial. She didn't pretend to be superhuman. She acknowledged fear, fatigue, uncertainty. But she also radiated something else – *peace*. A sense that life, even when heavy, was still worthy of celebration. She wore her scars with softness. She danced through the hard days with grace. She was living proof that resilience doesn't have to roar. Sometimes, it whispers – and still moves mountains.

Her personal life, too, reflected a deepening of joy. In 2008, she married John Easterling, an American entrepreneur and natural health advocate, in a quiet ceremony in Peru. Their bond was rooted in mutual care and a shared belief in the healing power of nature. Together, they built a life that was deeply intentional - gardens, greenhouses, music, and quiet mornings far from the noise of Hollywood.

And always, always - there was Chloe.

Olivia's daughter remained her centre, her mirror, her muse. Their bond, forged long before illness or fame ever intervened, remained steady. Over the years, they would perform together, advocate together, laugh together. For all the lights Olivia stood under, the one she shined for most was her daughter.

As the 2010s unfolded, Olivia faced recurrences of her cancer, including a metastasis to her spine. The headlines returned. The worry crept back. But Olivia never lost her warmth. Never let her illness define her narrative. She would acknowledge the reality, yes - but then she'd sing anyway. Garden anyway. Love anyway.

That was her real legacy. Not the records. Not even the films. But the way she kept choosing joy.

Because Olivia Newton-John, at her core, was never just a performer. She was

a giver. Of voice. Of time. Of strength. She used her fame not as a shield, but as a lantern - one she passed to others to light their own way through the dark.

And in doing so, she gave the world something rarer than a platinum album or a box office smash.

She gave us courage.

8

Grace and Gratitude

"*Love is letting go of fear / Love is letting go of doubt...*"

There's a unique kind of freedom that comes after the storm - the calm clarity of having nothing left to prove, and everything left to give. That's the Olivia Newton-John the world got to know in the final decades of her life. Not the rising star, not the chart-topper or screen siren, but the woman who had already been all of those things and now stood contentedly in her own light. It was softer. Deeper. But no less brilliant.

Throughout the 2000s and 2010s, Olivia never stopped singing. She didn't need to chase trends or top the Billboard charts. Instead, she made music that *meant* something. Albums like *Grace and Gratitude*, *Stronger Than Before*, and *Liv On* weren't created for mass appeal - they were acts of service. Personal, spiritual, and full of healing. These weren't records made to sell. They were made to soothe. To comfort. To *honour*.

Grace and Gratitude, in particular, became something of a compass for Olivia's fans - a serene, meditative collection of songs written in the aftermath of her cancer recovery and spiritual transformation. With lyrics that leaned into forgiveness, surrender, and quiet strength, Olivia offered listeners a space to breathe. No glitter. No power belts. Just presence. It was the sound of someone fully at peace with herself.

And then, just when you thought she might stay in that gentle lane forever, Olivia reminded us she could still bring the fun. Over the years, she dabbled joyfully in duets and reinventions, often with a wink to her own legacy. In 2010, she re-recorded "Physical" with Jane Lynch for *Glee*, complete with workout video parody and neon nostalgia. It was camp. It was cheeky. And it showed that Olivia could laugh at herself without ever losing an ounce of dignity.

The *Glee* cameo wasn't just a throwaway moment - it reignited a cultural love for Olivia among a new generation. Teens who hadn't yet seen *Grease* or skated through *Xanadu* now knew her as the woman in the leotard bringing the house down with Sue Sylvester. Olivia wasn't just a legend. She was *relevant*. Again.

In 2015, she teamed up with fellow cancer survivors Amy Sky and Beth Nielsen Chapman for the album *Liv On* - a moving, intimate project that spoke directly to grief, loss, and healing. It was less about performance and more about presence. Songs like "Stone in My Pocket" and "Don't Know What to Say" felt like open arms. These were lullabies for the heartbroken. And Olivia's voice, matured and mellowed by time, wrapped around each note like a blessing.

She continued to perform live, too - her Las Vegas residency was a love-in, a place where fans from every era came to sway and sing along. It wasn't a spectacle. It was a celebration. Olivia didn't need pyrotechnics or backup dancers. She needed only a mic, a smile, and a song. And when she sang "Hopelessly Devoted to You," the years melted away. She didn't chase her past - she carried it like a favourite melody.

But Olivia also embraced the present. She collaborated with daughter Chloe on music that was both playful and poignant, sharing their bond with the world in harmonies that said more than any interview could. She worked on charity albums, Christmas specials, and intimate performances that brought joy wherever they landed. She didn't *need* to work anymore. But she still chose to.

Because that was Olivia's quiet truth: she loved giving. She loved connecting. Not just with audiences, but with *people*. Whether it was a fan at a meet-and-greet, a fellow artist backstage, or a child in treatment at her cancer centre - Olivia showed up. Fully. With grace.

There was also her deepening environmental and animal rights advocacy. A longtime vegetarian and nature lover, she championed causes that reflected her values: compassion, stewardship, and sustainability. Her Gaia Retreat & Spa in Australia became more than a business - it was an extension of her soul. A sanctuary. A place to heal. Just like her music.

In these later years, Olivia's interviews became more reflective, her words tinged with the wisdom of someone who had danced through fame, fear, and transformation. She spoke of love as the only lasting thing. Of letting go. Of choosing peace over pain. And she always did so with that same luminous calm that had first captivated the world decades earlier.

Even as her cancer returned and spread, Olivia refused to let it dim her. She acknowledged it, yes – but she didn't dwell. She continued to sing, to walk in her garden, to laugh with Chloe, to beam with John. She chose life, again and again. Not because it was easy, but because it was *hers*. She didn't posture as a warrior. She simply lived – bravely, honestly, beautifully.

In a world that constantly tries to package celebrity into clickbait and spectacle, Olivia remained a rare thing: a star who never lost her softness. Who never hardened under pressure. Who never stopped being kind.

She gave the world decades of music. Countless performances. Infinite moments of joy. But what she offered most consistently, most enduringly, was *herself*. Fully, quietly, completely.

And in those final years – golden, grateful, graceful – Olivia Newton-John didn't just remind us who she was.

She reminded us who *we* could be.

9

A Little More Love

"*Where did my heart go? When did it lose the way? How did I give you all my soul?*"

When a voice as tender, enduring, and beloved as Olivia Newton-John's finally fades into silence, it doesn't really leave. It lingers - in melody, in memory, in the quiet moments where a song suddenly comes on and brings a wave of warmth that catches you off guard. That's what Olivia left behind. Not a catalogue. Not a brand. But a *feeling*. A softness that survived the spotlight. A spirit that lived in every verse she ever sang.

In the weeks and months following her passing on August 8, 2022, the world responded with an outpouring of affection that was both immediate and overwhelmingly heartfelt. Tributes came from all corners - fellow artists, friends, politicians, cancer survivors, fans who had grown up watching her skate across a disco-lit soundstage or sing about summer nights and hopeless devotion. No one needed reminding of who she was. The love came because we all already knew. We had felt it. For decades.

From her homeland in Australia to the Hollywood Hills, Olivia's impact was honoured in ways that felt less like ceremony and more like family remembrance. Buildings were lit in soft pink. Concerts paused for dedications. On social media, memories flooded in - stories of kindness at backstage doors, handwritten letters of encouragement from Olivia to complete strangers, nurses who recalled her calm presence during surprise hospital visits, young singers who remembered being told by their mums, "This is who you want to be like." She wasn't just admired. She was *loved*. With the kind of affection reserved for people who always gave more than they took.

Her Grease co-stars spoke with tearful reverence. John Travolta, whose chemistry with Olivia defined an era, offered one of the most moving tributes of all. He called her "his Sandy" and thanked her for making all of our lives better. It wasn't a line for the press. It was the truth. Olivia had that rare quality - the ability to feel familiar, even to those who never met her. She wasn't distant. She was *close*. She sang like someone who saw you.

The music world responded too, not with chart-topping tributes, but with performances soaked in reverence. Cover versions of "I Honestly Love You" and "Magic" filled memorials and charity shows, not as attempts to match her delivery, but as homages to the emotional honesty she brought to every line. You couldn't mimic Olivia. You could only honour her by being as open-hearted as she always was.

In Australia, plans quickly moved to create permanent tributes. The Olivia Newton-John Cancer Wellness & Research Centre in Melbourne, already a beacon of hope, became something more -

a living legacy. Donations poured in. Patients and staff shared their stories. Her name, already on the building, took on new weight. It stood not just for the celebrity who founded it, but for the woman who had walked its halls, held its hands, and made sure wellness included the *whole*person - mind, body, spirit, and heart.

There was talk, too, of posthumous honours. State funeral offers. Public statues. Tribute albums. But perhaps the most powerful legacy Olivia left wasn't made of marble or medals. It was something quieter. It was the countless lives she touched in private - the people she helped heal, the fans she lifted through loss, the communities she supported when the cameras weren't rolling. Olivia didn't need a stage to matter. She mattered *because* she never needed one.

And through it all, her music kept playing. On the radio. In shopping centres. In cars and kitchens and weddings and nursing homes. Her voice - always so crystalline, so comforting - seemed to take on new resonance. Songs that once felt nostalgic now felt eternal. "Hopelessly Devoted to You" didn't just conjure prom dresses and pastel ribbons anymore - it conjured gratitude. "Have You Never Been Mellow" asked something deeper. "Physical" now felt like a celebration of life, of movement, of the beautiful boldness of simply *being here*.

In the months after her passing, something else happened too - younger generations discovered her, really discovered her, for the first time. Not through *Grease* or retro playlists, but through TikToks, tribute videos, documentaries. The world re-learned what it had briefly forgotten: that Olivia Newton-John was not a relic of the past, but a timeless artist, a modern icon wrapped in warmth, strength, and sincerity.

And what a gift that is – to be remembered not just for the songs, but for the *singer*. For the way she made people feel safe. Seen. Soothed. Olivia wasn't just a soundtrack to people's lives. She was a light within them.

Perhaps that's the truest measure of legacy. Not the awards, though there were many. Not the headlines or the sales. But the space someone occupies in the hearts they touched. Olivia Newton-John didn't command rooms. She entered them gently. She didn't chase stardom. She let it find her, and then shared it with everyone else. She moved through the world with grace – not the kind that demands applause, but the kind that leaves a trace long after the song has ended.

She taught us that being tender was a form of strength. That softness could survive the storm. That joy was always worth reaching for, even in the darkest hour. And she did it all not by pretending to be perfect, but by being perfectly *human*.

That's why we keep playing her songs. That's why the tributes haven't stopped. Because Olivia Newton-John gave us a little more love – and it's still echoing, still blooming, still lifting us when we need it most.

10

Heartstrings and Halos

"*Love is all we need to get us through...*"

When a voice as pure as Olivia Newton-John's threads its way into the collective soul, it doesn't stay confined to the radio waves or the golden haze of nostalgia. It moves. It travels. It seeps into the hearts and harmonies of future performers, reshaping the way people understand pop, presence, and the subtle power of sincerity. Olivia's influence wasn't about mimicry or style theft - it was about possibility. She gave permission to be gentle in a world that often rewards volume. She proved that a whisper can hit harder than a scream, that sweetness can carry steel, and that emotion - *real*, unfiltered feeling - was always in fashion.

Across generations, Olivia's fingerprints are all over pop culture, though often in ways that shimmer rather than shout. You can hear her in the breathy phrasing of Kylie Minogue's early ballads, in the ethereal honesty of Natalie Imbruglia's *Torn*, in the sun-drenched harmonies of Delta Goodrem's hopeful choruses. All three women - fellow Australian exports, each carving their own path - have credited Olivia not just as a musical idol, but as a guiding light. Someone who showed what it looked like to lead with grace and succeed without cruelty.

Kylie in particular often called Olivia a trailblazer, citing her influence both vocally and personally. There was an elegance to the way Olivia navigated fame - that balance of humility and stardust - that resonated with artists who wanted longevity without losing themselves. In the 2010s, when Olivia joined Kylie onstage for a cheeky "Physical" moment during Mardi Gras, it wasn't just a nostalgia nod - it was a queen welcoming another into the lineage.

But Olivia's reach wasn't limited to fellow Australians. Across the Atlantic, artists like Mariah Carey and Christina Aguilera borrowed from Olivia's control and clarity. They may have added riffs and vocal gymnastics of their own, but the emotional core - the ability to sit inside a lyric and *mean it* - was pure Olivia. She was a masterclass in restraint. And in an era that increasingly celebrates vocal acrobatics, Olivia's style remains a reminder that sometimes the strongest performance is the quietest one.

And then there are the drag queens - artists of transformation, expression, and bold beauty - who embraced Olivia not just as a muse, but as a mirror. She offered more than just leotards and Sandy struts. She offered *iconography*. From *Grease* sing-alongs to *Xanadu*-themed pageants, her songs became anthems of self-discovery and playful power. On shows like *RuPaul's Drag Race*, Olivia's tracks - particularly "Hopelessly Devoted to You" and "Magic" - have been lip-synced not just with flair, but with real emotional weight. Drag artists often choose songs that let them *feel* – and few voices conjure as much feeling as Olivia's.

Her work, especially in the LGBTQ+ community, was embraced not because it was radical, but because it was *welcoming.* Olivia didn't position herself as a diva above the crowd. She stood within it. Her warmth, her openness, her unwavering support of love in all its forms made her feel like family. She was, in the truest sense, an ally before the term became fashionable. And fans noticed. Still do.

In the world of musical theatre, too, Olivia's legacy stretches long and bright. Productions of *Grease* – and there are *always* productions of *Grease* – continue to base their interpretation of Sandy more on Olivia's version than the Broadway original. That final transformation scene? The black pants, the big hair, the suggestive strut? That's all Olivia. She redefined the character, giving her a softness that never quite left, even in her boldest moment. Directors and performers still chase that balance – the sweetness and the steel – because Olivia did it so effortlessly, so humanly.

Outside of performance, her influence extended into the world of wellness, where her holistic approach to health set a template many now follow. Long before it was mainstream to talk about gut health, mindfulness, plant-based diets, or complementary cancer therapies, Olivia was doing it – and doing it with intelligence, compassion, and zero smugness. She didn't claim to have all the answers. She simply shared what helped her, and trusted others to find their way. That kind of honesty is rare in any industry – and even rarer in one so obsessed with image.

You see, Olivia's influence wasn't just about how people *sounded*. It was about how they *were*. The softness. The generosity. The unshakeable calm in the face of storms. You can't bottle that. You can't choreograph it. But artists across generations have tried to follow it - not by copying her, but by letting themselves be *more themselves*. Because Olivia proved that being real wasn't a liability. It was her secret weapon.

Her final collaborations and guest appearances - from duet albums to TV tributes - showed just how much affection her peers had for her. She was invited not out of obligation or nostalgia, but because people wanted her energy in the room. When Dolly Parton recorded a posthumous duet of "Jolene" with Olivia, it felt less like a marketing move and more like a long-awaited embrace between two women who had always understood each other - icons of kindness, toughness, and timeless appeal.

And that's really what Olivia gave the world: a *model*. Not just for singing, or acting, or reinventing. But for being. For showing up fully, joyfully, and without ego. For making softness a strength, and for reminding us all that light can be *fierce*.

Her influence isn't always obvious - it doesn't walk into a room with a spotlight. It arrives like her voice always did: gentle, warm, undeniable. It's in the pauses between verses, the glance before the key change, the decision to say something kind when you could say something clever. It's in the singer who holds back, the artist who listens, the celebrity who keeps their feet on the ground. It's in all of us who heard her once and *felt something shift*.

Because Olivia Newton-John wasn't just a muse. She was a map.

And the road she charted still leads exactly where it always did – straight to the heart.

11

I Honestly Love You

"Maybe I hang around here a little more than I should / We both know I've got somewhere else to go..."

As the world around her kept spinning - faster, louder, forever chasing the next viral moment - Olivia Newton-John began to slow her steps. Not out of retreat, and certainly not out of fear, but because she had learned, deeply and quietly, the truth of something her lyrics had always hinted at: that the best parts of life aren't loud. They're found in stillness. In connection. In presence. And in those final years, Olivia chose to live in the centre of that stillness.

She spent more and more time at her ranch in Southern California, surrounded by eucalyptus trees, herbs, laughter, and love. The outside world, with its flashing lights and noise, could wait. What mattered now was mornings with John. Afternoons with Chloe. Moments of softness with her animals, her garden, her memories. She didn't disappear - she simply grounded herself in the things that gave her peace.

By this time, Olivia was navigating her third major battle with cancer – this time metastatic, having spread to her spine. It was the kind of diagnosis that comes with unspoken timelines. But Olivia, ever the quiet rebel, refused to live in countdowns. She didn't focus on endings. She focused on *being.* She spoke openly about her pain, yes, but also about her joy – the walks she could still take, the meals she still enjoyed, the people she still cherished. Every day was a gift, she said. And she meant it.

She continued to record music, even as her physical energy waned. She found strength in harmonies, healing in melodies. Her voice – older now, but no less rich – seemed to carry even more meaning with each passing year. There was no need to belt, no need to impress. Just truth, pure and plain. Songs like "Window in the Wall," a duet with Chloe, felt like closing chapters of a novel written in love. And the lyrics – about healing divisions, about unity – rang out like a whisper of hope in a noisy, fractured world.

That was always Olivia's way. To soften where others hardened. To open where others closed. She didn't pretend to be unafraid. She simply refused to live afraid.

As tributes and honours continued to arrive – lifetime achievement awards, honorary doctorates, global acknowledgments of her activism – Olivia received them with the same grace she always had. Grateful, humbled, but never grand. She knew who she was. And she knew what mattered.

In the final months, her presence became quieter, more limited. But even then, she found ways to connect – video messages for fans, birthday wishes, short songs shared online. Her smile, while slower to arrive, never disappeared. She kept showing up, however she could. Not because she *had* to. Because she *wanted* to. Because the connection was still there - between her and the millions of people who had walked through life with her voice as their companion.

On August 8, 2022, Olivia passed away at her California home, surrounded by family and love. The news spread swiftly, but it didn't feel like shock. It felt like the ending of a beautiful song. Bittersweet. Inevitable. And full of gratitude. The kind of farewell that aches and warms in equal measure.

In the days that followed, the world didn't just mourn her - it *celebrated* her. Her songs returned to the charts. Her films played in cinemas and living rooms alike. Candlelight vigils, tribute concerts, online memorials - all lit up with a kind of soft joy. Because even in death, Olivia had managed to remind people not to chase sadness, but to lean into love.

And the love was *everywhere*. From the Prime Minister of Australia to school choirs in small towns. From megastars who had once idolised her, to elderly fans who had grown up with her voice on vinyl. Everyone had a story. A moment. A song. Because Olivia had become more than a pop star or actress or advocate. She had become part of people's lives. A thread woven through memory, emotion, and time.

Her funeral, held privately with family, was quiet and personal. Just as she would've wanted. But in Australia, a public memorial followed - a celebration of life, broadcast with music and tributes and tears that shimmered with joy. Her family, friends, and fellow artists spoke not of her fame, but of her presence. Her ability to make anyone feel safe, heard, loved. Her refusal to let bitterness touch her, even when she had every reason to be angry with the world.

John Easterling, her husband, spoke of her faith in nature, her fierce compassion, and the way she found light in the darkest corners. Chloe spoke of the mother who never stopped being her biggest fan. And fans around the world lit candles, played her records, and whispered "I honestly love you" into the night, as though she might still hear it.

And maybe she does.

Because Olivia Newton-John's legacy isn't held in a museum. It's not confined to platinum records or framed movie posters. It lives in the soft parts of people. In the songs they play when they miss someone. In the words they say when they want to comfort a friend. In the way they choose peace over anger, hope over fear, grace over noise.

Her final message, shared just before her passing, was simple.

"Be kind. Stay grounded. Keep singing."

That's the Olivia Newton-John the world carries forward. The voice, yes. The beauty, of course. But mostly, the *heart*. She taught us that to be strong didn't mean being hard. That to be a star didn't mean burning others out. That to live a good life – a *true* life – was to love fully, give gently, and leave the world softer than you found it.

She honestly loved us.

And we, forever, love her back.

12

Don't Stop Believin'

"*Don't stop believin', hold on to that feelin'..."* - *from her 1976 hit, not just a Journey lyric*

There's something sacred about slipping an Olivia Newton-John record onto a turntable - or, let's be honest, queuing up a playlist with trembling thumbs. The music doesn't just *play* - it glows. And while the world may remember the big hits - the *Grease* duets, the spandex-era sparkle of "Physical" - there's a whole landscape behind those radio staples. A discography so rich, so quietly daring, it forms a kind of spiritual map. Not just of a career, but of a woman constantly evolving - not to keep up with trends, but to reflect her truth.

The journey began in the late '60s with gentle ripples of folk and country-pop. Olivia's debut solo album, *If Not for You* (1971), was like a postcard from a softer world - filled with acoustic strumming and warm vulnerability. The title track, a Bob Dylan cover by way of George Harrison, already revealed her uncanny ability to turn borrowed lyrics into something deeply personal. You didn't feel like she was covering a song. You felt like she was uncovering it. Laying it bare. Singing it for you, and only you.

The early '70s were an outpouring of emotion and twang. Albums like *Olivia*

(1972) and *Let Me Be There* (1973) leaned into that Nashville sound, pairing her creamy vocals with steel guitar and gospel harmonies. But Olivia never sounded like she was putting on a country costume. She wasn't pretending. She was connecting. And America - deep in its post-hippie haze - couldn't get enough. "Let Me Be There" became a crossover hit, with its descending harmonies and easygoing optimism. For many, that was the gateway drug. From that point on, she was more than just another blonde with a pretty voice. She was *the* voice.

Then came *Have You Never Been Mellow* (1975), and mellow never sounded so mesmerizing. It was the first Olivia album that felt like its own ecosystem - the production airy and sun-drenched, the melodies wrapped in satin. It was country-pop, yes, but with a California shimmer. You could almost feel the breeze. You could almost close your eyes and drift.

But Olivia, ever evolving, wasn't about to stay in one genre. Her late '70s output - *Don't Stop Believin'* (1976), *Making a Good Thing Better* (1977) - saw her dabble in soft rock, disco flourishes, and lyrical introspection. The title track of *Don't Stop Believin'* isn't just a hidden gem - it's a manifesto. Not of ego, but of quiet endurance. Olivia wasn't making declarations. She was making invitations. Come with me, the songs seemed to say. We'll keep going, gently, always.

And then came the game-changer: *Totally Hot* (1978). Released in the wake of *Grease*'s global explosion, this album saw

Olivia channel a new kind of fire. The cover - black leather, fierce gaze, curls wild and untamed - was a visual announcement: the sweet girl had grown up. Tracks like "A Little More Love" and "Deeper Than the Night" still shimmered with pop melody, but they had a new edge. This was not rebellion for its own sake. This was evolution with purpose. Olivia didn't ditch the old self - she expanded her.

The early '80s brought her to the pop stratosphere. *Physical* (1981) wasn't just a hit - it was a *moment*. That title track, cheeky and daring, layered with synths and a wink, became her biggest global success. But to define that album by one track alone would be criminal. Songs like "Carried Away" and "Stranger's Touch" revealed a woman exploring the full spectrum of desire, playfulness, and vulnerability. She was bold, but never brash. Sexy, but never self-parodying. She understood something rare: that femininity didn't have to sacrifice depth for glamour. It could hold both.

From there, Olivia entered what many fans call her "dream trilogy." Albums like *Soul Kiss* (1985), *The Rumour* (1988), and *Warm and Tender* (1989) showed a woman willing to follow her muse - whether or not the charts followed her. *Soul Kiss* leaned into sultry synth-pop, all shimmering keyboards and breathy vocals. *The Rumour*, produced in part by Elton John, explored social issues - safe sex, global unity - long before they were pop topics. And *Warm and Tender*, a lullaby album for children, was a return to softness that never felt regressive. It was maternal. Deeply personal. A sonic quilt.

In the '90s and beyond, Olivia became even more fearless. *Gaia: One Woman's Journey* (1994) - written after her first cancer diagnosis – is perhaps her most autobiographical work. Songs like "Not Gonna Give In to It" and "Don't Cut Me Down" are raw, open-hearted, and meditative. Gone were the chart ambitions. In their place was a deep need to *express*. To heal. To *be*. Gaia was not a comeback – it was a spiritual unveiling.

That sense of quiet revelation carried through into her 2000s releases: *Indigo: Women of Song* (2004), a tribute to the female artists she adored; *Grace and Gratitude* (2006), a spiritual collection rooted in affirmation and healing; and *Liv On*(2016), her grief-soaked, hopeful collaboration with Amy Sky and Beth Nielsen Chapman. Each of these records felt like a gift – not a performance, but a presence. Olivia wasn't just singing *to* us. She was sitting *with* us.

Even her final recordings – duets with Chloe, guest vocals, special editions – carried that same warmth. Her voice, a little grainier now, still rang with clarity and soul. In every phase, she knew exactly who she was – not because she clung to a persona, but because she allowed herself to change.

For fans, her discography isn't just a setlist. It's a roadmap. A comfort blanket. A diary written in melody. It reminds us of who we were when we first heard her. And who we still want to be.

Don't stop believin'? We never did.

Not when it came to Olivia.

13

Twist of Fate

"*It's gonna be a strange twist of fate, telling me that heaven can wait...*" - from *Twist of Fate* (1983)

When people think of Olivia Newton-John on film, their minds inevitably drift to *Grease*. Sandy Olsson, the ingénue in pearls who turned into the woman in black, is an image so culturally embedded that it almost eclipses everything else. Yet Olivia's filmography tells a much broader story. It reveals a performer willing to play, to take risks, and to trust the camera the same way she trusted a melody - with openness, honesty, and that quietly radiant charm that made audiences feel safe in her world.

After *Grease* catapulted her into international superstardom, the offers flooded in. Studios wanted another musical, another romance, another spark of that Sandy magic. But Olivia, ever attuned to her own instincts, wasn't looking to repeat herself. She wanted to *grow* - and that journey took her to places the critics didn't always understand but fans still cherish decades later.

Her first major post-*Grease* outing was *Xanadu* (1980), that gloriously glitter-dusted fever dream where roller disco met Greek mythology. Olivia played Kira, a muse from Mount Olympus who inspires a struggling artist to create a nightclub of pure light and joy. It was a film that, even now, feels more like a hallucination than a Hollywood product. The plot made little sense, but it didn't need to. *Xanadu* was about feeling - the shimmer of music, the possibility of love, and the strange, electric optimism of the early '80s. Gene Kelly lent it gravitas, ELO filled the air with symphonic disco, and Olivia floated through it all like a celestial being in legwarmers.

Critics at the time dismissed it as kitsch, but something extraordinary happened in the years that followed: *Xanadu*became a cult classic. Its soundtrack went platinum, its visuals turned iconic, and fans - from theatre kids to drag performers - embraced it as a beacon of joy. Olivia, with her serene grace and light-up-the-room smile, gave the fantasy a soul. Even amidst the neon and the nonsense, she was *real*. That's her secret weapon on screen - sincerity that never feels forced.

Then, in 1983, came *Two of a Kind*. Reuniting with John Travolta should have been a surefire win - a second *Grease*, a guaranteed success. But Olivia and John, perhaps wisely, didn't try to recapture the past. Instead, they ventured into something stranger: a romantic fable wrapped in divine comedy. Olivia played Debbie, a bank teller caught up in a celestial wager between good and evil. The plot was biblical, bizarre, and brimming with charm in unexpected places.

Where critics saw confusion, fans saw chemistry. Olivia and Travolta had that rare on-screen alchemy - not just attraction, but affection. Their connection was softer this time, more adult.

Gone were the high school flirtations; in their place was a bond between two bruised souls daring to hope again. Olivia grounded the fantasy with emotional truth, turning what could have been pulp into something tender. And once again, when the film faltered, the music soared.

The *Two of a Kind* soundtrack was pure gold. "Twist of Fate," its flagship single, throbbed with urgency and light, a slick, pulsating anthem that gave Olivia another top ten hit. Her voice, sharper now, cut clean through the glossy production - confident, sexy, assured. Songs like "Livin' in Desperate Times" and "Take a Chance" (her duet with Travolta) echoed across dance floors and car radios, reminding the world that whatever the screen reception, Olivia the musician was untouchable.

By the 1990s, Olivia had begun to step away from Hollywood blockbusters and into smaller, more heartfelt projects. *A Mom for Christmas* (1990), a made-for-TV holiday movie, showed her leaning fully into her gentle, nurturing side. She played a department store mannequin brought to life to help a lonely girl rediscover joy. It was whimsical and warm - exactly the kind of film that would air on repeat through the festive season, comfortingly predictable yet impossible not to smile through. Olivia brought the role a softness that transcended the script. She didn't need CGI to perform magic. Her eyes did that all on their own.

Then came a turn that surprised everyone: *Sordid Lives* (2000). This wasn't light, sparkly Olivia. This was raw, smoky-voiced, small-town Olivia - playing Bitsy Mae Harling, a bar singer and ex-con in a Texan tragicomedy full of eccentric characters and secrets. She didn't headline it, but she didn't need to.

Her scenes carried a world-weary tenderness that earned her cult affection from an entirely new audience. The film itself became a Southern queer classic, and Olivia - never afraid to stand alongside her LGBTQ+ fans - leaned in with full-hearted authenticity. Her accompanying songs, including the tongue-in-cheek "Jack Daniels If You Please," revealed another layer of her musical soul: the country storyteller, the woman who could turn even heartache into honey.

Olivia's later screen work tended to blend her artistic identities. Concert films, charity appearances, and television cameos - like her brilliant *Glee* duet with Jane Lynch - allowed her to celebrate her past while winking at it, too. Few stars can parody their own legend without losing dignity, but Olivia made self-awareness look like grace. She never treated nostalgia as a trap; she treated it as a gift.

Looking back, her cinematic journey feels like an extension of her music: always heartfelt, sometimes underappreciated, and deeply human. She wasn't chasing Oscars or critical validation. She was chasing connection. Whether floating through *Xanadu*, sparring with Travolta among angels, or singing in a smoky Texan bar, she carried that same light. The light of someone who believed in joy, no matter how improbable the setting.

When Olivia sang "It's gonna be a strange twist of fate," she might as well have been describing her screen career - unpredictable, peculiar, occasionally overlooked, but always filled with heart. The movies didn't make her a star. She made *them* shine brighter.

14

Soul Kiss

"*I see a hunger in your eyes, I feel the thunder inside...*" - from *Soul Kiss* (1985)

For most of the world, Olivia Newton-John would always be the sunny girl with the feathered hair and the golden voice. The clean-cut Sandy, the pure-voiced songbird, the wholesome pop queen whose smile could melt radio dials. But by the mid-1980s, that image was starting to feel more like a costume than a skin. Olivia was a grown woman. A mother. A performer who had lived through global fame, personal reinvention, and creative risk. The Olivia of *Soul Kiss* wasn't here to play sweet anymore. She was here to smoulder.

Released in 1985, *Soul Kiss* was Olivia's twelfth studio album and, by all accounts, her most daring. It came three years after *Physical* - the record that had already begun chipping away at her squeaky-clean image with its sweaty, tongue-in-cheek sexuality. But *Soul Kiss* didn't just chip away. It took a sledgehammer to the idea of what an Olivia Newton-John album should sound like, look like, *feel* like. Gone were the innocent curls and pastel tones. In their place? Slick lipstick, bedroom eyes, and a voice that whispered, purred, and demanded your attention.

The lead single - the album's title track - arrived like a velvet revolution. "Soul Kiss" was synth-heavy, breathy, hypnotic. Olivia's delivery was all sultry hush and subtle suggestion. The chorus, layered in sensual harmonies, wrapped itself around listeners like perfume in a darkened room. This wasn't a wink or a tease. It was desire, direct and unfiltered. And it surprised people. Olivia - the girl who once sang about hopeless devotion - now sang about hunger and thunder, about lips and longing. Some fans were scandalised. Others were thrilled. But no one could say she was standing still.

The album artwork told its own story. Photographed by the legendary Helmut Newton, Olivia appeared more like a fashion-forward Bond girl than the sweet-faced girl from Melbourne. In one shot, she reclined in a men's blazer and tie, all shoulder pads and shadows. In another, she stared straight into the lens, lips parted, daring you to challenge her authority. This wasn't a woman asking for approval. This was a woman claiming space - elegant, commanding, and just a little dangerous.

Critically, *Soul Kiss* met a cool reception. Some reviewers couldn't reconcile the album's sleek eroticism with the Olivia they thought they knew. Others criticised the production as over-stylised, the lyrics as too soft-focus. But what those critiques missed was the point: *Soul Kiss* wasn't trying to fit a mold. It was trying to break one. It was Olivia, ever polite but never passive, saying: I contain multitudes.

Musically, the album plays like a time capsule of mid-'80s pop sophistication. Tracks like "Toughen Up" brought a percussive edge, while "Queen of the Publication" was a biting satire of tabloid culture, delivered with sly knowingness. "Emotional Tangle" leaned into pulsing bass lines and echoing vocals, conjuring the neon-lit loneliness of nightclubs and city streets. Throughout it all, Olivia's voice remained the anchor - softer now, but no less powerful. Her vocals shimmered, floated, sometimes sighed. She didn't belt. She *invited* you closer.

Some songs didn't chart high, but they lingered. "The Right Moment," co-written by Simon Climie (of Climie Fisher), is a ballad of aching patience, where Olivia stretches every line like silk pulled across candlelight. "Moth to a Flame" simmers with restrained tension, a metaphor that plays out in every beat. There's a maturity to these songs - emotionally and vocally - that hinted at the artist behind the icon. Not just a performer, but a woman fully inhabiting her skin.

What *Soul Kiss* also revealed, perhaps more than any album before it, was Olivia's quiet bravery. It's easy to forget now, but in 1985, female artists were often punished for pivoting away from innocence. The Madonna-MTV era was rising, and women who owned their sensuality were either celebrated or scorned - rarely both. Olivia had already dabbled in this with "Physical," but *Soul Kiss* pushed further, deeper. It wasn't cheeky anymore. It was honest. Intimate. And entirely on her terms.

In hindsight, it's tempting to see *Soul Kiss* as a commercial misstep - it didn't match the chart-topping highs of her earlier work, and radio stations seemed unsure of what to do with this new, grown-up Olivia. But to define success by numbers alone would be to miss its deeper legacy. This album laid the groundwork for the next phase of her artistry - one in which she'd speak openly about vulnerability, womanhood, and emotional strength. *Soul Kiss* was less about seduction and more about sovereignty.

And for the fans who followed Olivia not for her chart placements but for her *spirit*, the album remains a favourite. It's the sound of a woman testing her boundaries, not because she had to – but because she *wanted* to. It's a collection of songs that shimmer in low light, best listened to with headphones and wine, somewhere between midnight and memory.

Perhaps the most telling thing about *Soul Kiss* is that Olivia never seemed to regret it. She didn't bury it in interviews or laugh it off. She wore it like she wore that Helmut Newton blazer – unapologetically, elegantly, with eyes wide open. It was a kiss for the soul, not the charts. And for those who truly listened, it landed exactly where it needed to.

15

The Right Moment

"*Now is the right time, the right moment... the light is falling into place.*" - from *The Right Moment* (1985)

After the bold sensuality of *Soul Kiss*, Olivia Newton-John could've doubled down on reinvention. She could've chased the charts, leaned further into the synthetic gloss of the mid-'80s, and shaped herself into a permanent fixture of pop radio. But Olivia wasn't wired for reinvention without purpose. She never moved with the trends - she moved with her heart. And what her heart wanted now was something far from the studio lights and fashion shoots. She wanted stillness. She wanted space. She wanted home.

In June 1986, Olivia gave birth to her daughter, Chloe Rose Lattanzi. It was, by all accounts, a seismic shift. Fame had once been the constant drumbeat in her life - shows, interviews, red carpets, releases. But the arrival of Chloe quieted that rhythm. Olivia didn't just become a mother. She *chose* motherhood. Chose to step away from the spotlight's intensity and into something slower, deeper, more personal. She didn't announce a retirement or stage an exit. She just *slipped* into the next phase of her life, as gently as a curtain falling between acts.

And yet, even in this quieter era, she was still creating. Music hadn't abandoned her - it had simply softened. Her vocals grew warmer, more introspective. You could hear it in songs like "The Right Moment," a haunting ballad buried in the folds of *Soul Kiss* that now seemed to echo the next chapter more than the last. It was Olivia stripped back - no glitter, no pose, just feeling. And what she was feeling, increasingly, was a pull toward meaning. Toward purpose. Toward healing.

Throughout the late '80s and early '90s, her music took on this subtler shape. Albums like *Warm and Tender* (1989) stepped fully into motherhood's embrace. Designed as a children's album, *Warm and Tender* was more than lullabies - it was a love letter. Olivia's voice, always crystal, now carried a maternal hush. She sang for the next generation, not the charts. It was the kind of project a woman makes not for applause, but for memory - something her daughter could hold, something parents could trust, something that spoke not to the world's noise but to its hope.

It was around this time that Olivia began to reimagine her identity outside of fame. She started *Koala Blue*, a fashion and lifestyle brand co-founded with her friend and former business partner Pat Carroll. What began as a small boutique selling Australian-themed clothing became an international venture, its blue-and-white branding showing up in malls from Sydney to Los Angeles. It was a savvy business move, sure, but more than that, it was an extension of Olivia's spirit - welcoming, clean, stylish without being flashy. For a while, the brand soared.

But eventually, like many passion projects launched in the boom of the '80s, it faltered. Koala Blue went into bankruptcy in the early '90s, a quiet disappointment Olivia rarely dwelled on. She'd taken a swing - and more importantly, she'd followed her instincts. Failure didn't scare her. Inauthenticity did.

The early '90s also marked a return to film, but not in the way most would expect. In 1990, she starred in *A Mom for Christmas*, a made-for-TV movie that aired on NBC and became a surprise holiday staple. Olivia played a mannequin brought to life to help a young girl rediscover the spirit of Christmas. It sounds whimsical - and it was - but there was something else shimmering beneath the surface. A tenderness. A vulnerability. Olivia wasn't just playing magic - she *embodied* it. That's what made her on-screen presence so enduring. She never had to push. She just *was*.

And behind the scenes, something more profound was unfolding. Olivia's worldview was expanding, subtly but significantly. She began engaging more openly in environmental causes and animal welfare. The girl who'd grown up in the wilds of Australia was reconnecting with nature in a deeper way - not just as scenery, but as a system, something sacred. Her music, too, began reflecting these values. There was less gloss, more earth. Less performance, more presence.

Then, in 1992, everything changed.

Olivia was diagnosed with breast cancer. It was a revelation that rocked her world - and the world of her fans. This woman who had been the picture of health, who had glowed on stage and screen, was suddenly face-to-face with mortality. But Olivia didn't retreat into silence. She met her diagnosis with the same grace that had defined every step of her career – with honesty, courage, and a desire to use even this as a way to help others.

Treatment was grueling, and she took time away to recover. But the experience lit a new fire in her – not the fire of ambition, but the fire of purpose. She would become an advocate. A symbol not of survival, but of healing. She spoke publicly about her journey, not for attention, but for connection. If her story could help even one woman catch her cancer early, it was worth every headline.

And so, from this moment – this right moment – Olivia's life shifted again. Music would continue, yes, but as a *vessel*. A means for storytelling, healing, and hope. Gone were the chart games and image wars. What remained was a woman with a story, and the heart to share it.

Looking back, the late '80s and early '90s may seem like Olivia's quietest years. Fewer hits. Fewer headlines. But they were, in truth, her most formative. They were the years in which Olivia became Olivia – not just the star, but the soul. She embraced her humanity, her limitations, her truth. She stepped off the stage and into life. And in doing so, she found something more lasting than applause. She found peace.

Because the right moment isn't always the loudest one. Sometimes, it's the moment you stop running. The moment you hold your child. The moment you let go of what the world expects and embrace what your spirit needs.

For Olivia Newton-John, *this* was that moment.

16

Gaia

"*I am a child of the universe, I am a child of the Earth...*" - from *Gaia: One Woman's Journey* (1994)

When Olivia Newton-John emerged from her battle with breast cancer in the early 1990s, she didn't just return to music - she *transformed* it. The glossy pop princess of the past didn't vanish, but she gave way to someone richer, braver, and infinitely more grounded. That transformation arrived in the form of *Gaia: One Woman's Journey*, a 1994 album that stands apart from every other record in her discography - not because it sold the most or spun out hit singles, but because it came straight from her soul.

To call *Gaia* an album almost feels too small. It's a confession. A prayer. A reclamation. Written entirely by Olivia herself - a first - this wasn't just a collection of songs. It was a roadmap through pain, survival, and self-discovery. After a career shaped in large part by the visions of others - producers, labels, Hollywood studios - *Gaia* was all Olivia. Every lyric, every melody, every breath.

She recorded the album in Australia's lush Byron Bay, where rainforest meets ocean and time seems to slow into stillness. The natural world became part of the music itself. You can almost hear the wind through eucalyptus, the morning birdsong, the rhythmic hush of waves between notes. And at the centre of it all: Olivia, newly raw, newly real, pouring her story into every line.

The opening track, *Trust Yourself*, sets the tone like a mantra. It's gentle but determined, a quiet reminder that strength isn't about force - it's about faith. Olivia's voice is stripped back, intimate, unadorned. She's not performing anymore - she's *sharing.* And that vulnerability continues through the album like a river.

Why Me is one of the most heartbreakingly honest songs she ever recorded. It's a question asked without bitterness, just quiet bewilderment - the way someone might speak into the ceiling on a sleepless night. And then comes *Not Gonna Give In to It*, the closest the album comes to a fight song. But even here, Olivia doesn't rage. She *resolves.* Her strength isn't loud, it's lived-in. Steady. Unshakable.

One of the most powerful aspects of *Gaia* is how seamlessly it weaves together Olivia's personal healing and her deepening relationship with the Earth. The title track is almost elemental - a love song to the planet, yes, but also to the body, to womanhood, to life itself. She sings, "I am a child of the universe," and you believe her. This isn't a slogan. It's a truth she earned through struggle and reflection.

And while some may have expected a soft, folksy record, *Gaia* is far from delicate. It's layered and lush, with flutes, acoustic guitars, tribal percussion, and rich vocal harmonies. The production, though rooted in nature, is sophisticated. Tracks like *Don't Cut Me Down* and *No Matter What You Do* are quietly searing - beautifully melodic, but laced with emotional fire. Olivia had never sounded more in control, more honest, more *herself*.

Don't Cut Me Down, in particular, is a standout - an environmental plea disguised as a personal lament. Whether she's singing to a tree or to a person who's failed to see her fully, the pain is real. "You never look my way," she sings, and it lands like a quiet accusation. It's activism via intimacy.

What's remarkable about *Gaia* is how little it cared for commercial approval. Olivia had no intention of chasing radio play or chart placement. She didn't need to. She was telling the truth. That was the goal. This wasn't about trends - it was about testimony.

And for those who listened - really listened - *Gaia* became a touchstone. It wasn't just an album you played; it was an album you turned to. For comfort, for courage, for clarity. It became part of healing playlists, yoga sessions, late-night drives, and sunlit mornings. It found its audience not in numbers, but in depth.

Critics who had once dismissed Olivia as too safe or too saccharine were forced to re-evaluate. Here was an artist who had gone to the edge - physically, emotionally - and come back bearing something transcendent. The sweetness in her voice now carried weight. The grace had grit behind it. This was a woman who had stared down her own mortality and chosen to sing back to it.

And it's worth noting: *Gaia* wasn't just a personal album - it was also a beginning. From this point forward, Olivia would align more and more with environmental causes, cancer research, wellness, and holistic health. She wasn't just talking about healing anymore. She was *living* it. Building centres, funding research, and becoming a beacon for anyone navigating illness or uncertainty. *Gaia* was the soundtrack to that mission - and, in a way, the blueprint.

In the years that followed, Olivia's music would continue in this more organic, heartfelt direction. But nothing ever quite matched the spiritual resonance of *Gaia*. It stands alone. A singular achievement. Not her most famous album. Not her most played. But without doubt, her *most true*.

For fans who had danced to "Physical" and swooned to "Hopelessly Devoted," *Gaia* offered something deeper. It said: Olivia is still here. Not just the voice, but the woman. Stronger. Wiser. Awake. And, above all, grateful.

Because when the world falls away - when fame quiets, when illness comes, when image no longer matters - what remains is the soul. And in *Gaia*, Olivia Newton-John gave us hers

17

A Little More Love

"*Where did my heart go wrong? Tell me, tell me...*" - from *A Little More Love* (1978)

By the late 1990s, Olivia Newton-John had travelled farther - emotionally, spiritually, even sonically - than most artists dare to go. She had been a country ingénue, a disco queen, a pop powerhouse, a cancer survivor, a wellness advocate, and a nature-loving folk singer. And now, in this more settled phase of her life, there was still one thread pulling everything together: love. Not the glossy kind sung on the radio. Not the cinematic kind played out on screen. But something gentler, deeper. Olivia had reached a place where her creative output was less about reinvention and more about intention - sharing, serving, soothing. She wasn't chasing trends. She was offering peace.

She could've slipped away quietly. Many of her peers had. But Olivia's spirit didn't lean toward retreat - it leaned toward relevance, not through flash, but through connection. Her voice remained unchanged in tone, but it gained a new dimension:

wisdom. You could hear it in every note she sang in the late '90s. She had seen the fragility of life up close and was now using her platform not to escape the world, but to help heal it.

Much of her energy turned toward service. In 1992, the same year she went public with her breast cancer diagnosis, Olivia became a fierce advocate for early detection and patient support. But it was never about celebrity awareness campaigns or photo ops. It was about *people*. She spoke openly, intimately, with honesty that cut through stigma. And she backed up her words with action, eventually founding the Olivia Newton-John Cancer Wellness & Research Centre in Melbourne - a place of science, but also of sanctuary. Patients could access cutting-edge treatment alongside holistic therapies like music, massage, and meditation. It was the embodiment of everything Olivia had come to believe: that healing is not just physical, but emotional and spiritual too.

And still, she sang.

In 1998, she released *Back with a Heart*, a country-tinged return that bridged her earliest sounds with the woman she'd become. There was something poetic in it - the girl who'd left Australia with a guitar and a dream now returning to country music with eyes wide open and heart fully engaged. The album didn't shout. It *glowed*. Lead single *I Honestly Love You* - her 1974 classic - was reimagined as a duet with Babyface, his silky harmonies folding around her familiar softness like a warm shawl. The song had once been a tender whisper from a young woman unsure of how to express love. Now, it was something else entirely - a reaffirmation, seasoned with experience and loss. Time had weathered the edges of her voice ever so slightly, but it only made the song land deeper. This wasn't nostalgia. It was evolution.

Olivia never courted irony. She didn't dabble in reinvention for the sake of headlines. But her choices in this era often carried a quiet boldness. Like appearing on *Dharma & Greg* or voicing a singing trout on *The Man from Snowy River*soundtrack. She leaned into joy. Into silliness. Into collaboration. She didn't take herself too seriously, which only made people take her more seriously.

But perhaps the most quietly radical thing she did in the late '90s and early 2000s was *stay*. Stay present. Stay visible. Stay giving. In an industry that often tells women – especially women past a certain age – that their value expires, Olivia remained luminous. She didn't fight age. She embraced it. She glowed through it. That ageless smile, those kind eyes, that voice like eucalyptus honey – they became symbols not just of her music, but of her ethos.

She lent that voice to causes as often as she did to songs. Charity concerts. Benefit albums. Appearances for cancer research, environmental awareness, animal rights. She showed up, again and again, often without fanfare. And when she did sing, it was with that same intention: to lift spirits. She wasn't trying to top charts anymore – she was trying to *touch hearts*.

In 2002, Olivia released 2, a duets album that felt more like a celebration of friendship than a record. Collaborating with artists like Tina Arena, Darren Hayes, and Billy Thorpe, she traversed musical styles with the warmth of someone inviting you into their living room. Her voice never dominated – it *blended.* She made space. That was Olivia's way. Whether she was harmonising with a fellow artist or listening to a fan's cancer story at a fundraiser, she always *made space.*

It's easy to underestimate the power of such softness in a music industry built on bravado. But Olivia's strength had never been loud. It had been *lasting.* She was a lesson in grace. A masterclass in how to evolve not by outrunning your past, but by folding it into your present.

And through it all – through motherhood, through advocacy, through reinvention – there was always that thread of love. A little more love, given freely, without demand. You could hear it in every note. See it in every smile. Feel it in every cause she championed.

By the time the 2000s arrived, Olivia Newton-John had transcended the labels once used to define her. Singer. Actress. Star. She had become something else entirely: a presence. A comfort. A beacon.

And what's remarkable is that she did it not by reinventing herself – but by *returning* to herself. Again and again. With every album. Every stage. Every story shared.

A little more love, she gave. A little more light, she left behind.

18

Magic

"You have to believe we are magic – nothing can stand in our way..." – from *Magic* (1980)

Some stars burn fast and bright, vanishing into legend before the final curtain falls. But Olivia Newton-John? She shimmered. Not in a blaze, not in a flash – but with the kind of quiet radiance that lingers long after the house lights come up. Her final decades weren't about reinvention or comeback. They were about *glow*. A steady, golden glow that warmed everyone lucky enough to bask in it.

The Olivia of the 2000s and beyond had little to prove. Her place in pop history was secure. Grease remained a cultural phenomenon, *Physical* still pulsed through gym speakers everywhere, and even the most ironic hipsters had to admit that "Xanadu" was a total bop. But while others might've coasted on nostalgia, Olivia kept creating. Her later years were marked not by retreat, but by refinement. She chose her projects carefully, lived with intention, and channelled her time into things that truly mattered.

Music never left her. She just changed how she held it. Gone were the disco beats and radio hooks – in their place came lullabies, sacred chants, seasonal hymns, and healing mantras. Her 2006 album *Grace and Gratitude* – released first in partnership with a line of wellness products and later reissued in expanded form – felt less like an album and more like a spa for the soul. Tracks like *Let Go Let God* and *Instrument of Peace* weren't designed for airplay; they were gifts for quiet mornings and heavy hearts.

In these songs, Olivia wasn't trying to entertain. She was trying to ease. To soothe. To accompany people through illness, anxiety, grief – the everyday burdens that don't make headlines but leave deep marks. She became less a performer and more a *presence*. And her voice, always a balm, now carried the patina of lived experience. It was gentler, lower, worn in like a favourite sweater – and all the more beautiful for it.

Her concerts in these later years became less spectacle and more sanctuary. She still sang the hits – of course she did, and always with love – but now she paired *Magic* with messages of hope, followed *Physical* with heartfelt chats about healing. Audiences didn't just come to dance. They came to cry, to laugh, to feel seen. There was something sacred in the way she held a room – without ego, without fuss, just open-hearted and real.

And real she remained, even in the spotlight's glare. She continued to be remarkably candid about her long and evolving cancer journey. After her initial diagnosis in 1992, she would face recurrences in 2013 and again in 2017, when the disease spread to her sacrum. Yet she rarely spoke in terms of battle or defeat. She framed it as a journey. A process. Something to walk through with grace.

In one interview, she smiled gently and said, "We're all going to die at some point, that's the truth. So I try to enjoy every day." It wasn't bravado. It was peace. That was the magic of Olivia Newton-John - her ability to take life's hardest truths and alchemise them into something soft and shimmering.

Even as she slowed down physically, her creative spirit never waned. She recorded with her daughter, Chloe Lattanzi, their harmonies blending like lullabies passed down through generations. She released duets albums, reimagined classics, and appeared in projects that felt more like love letters than career moves. Each choice was deliberate. Each song, a thank-you.

Her philanthropy reached new heights too. The Olivia Newton-John Cancer Wellness & Research Centre became a beacon, not just for its cutting-edge treatment but for its holistic care model - music therapy, pet visits, art, meditation, counselling, community. It was her vision made real: healing as something whole and human. Not just surviving, but living. Loving. Laughing, even.

And Olivia laughed often. Her humour was famously dry, a little cheeky. She loved a good wink, a clever pun, a silly backstage moment. For all the reverence people placed on her - the goddess, the angel, the Earth Mother - she remained wonderfully grounded. She never put herself above others. Instead, she seemed to invite you into her light and say, *"Come as you are - we're all walking each other home."*

In her final public appearances, you could see the toll illness had taken. But you could also see the sparkle. That unmistakable Olivia gleam - not just in her eyes, but in her presence. She never dimmed. Even in pain. Even when it became clear that her journey might be nearing its close, she continued to offer encouragement. Gratitude. Love.

And when the news came, in August 2022, that Olivia Newton-John had passed away at her beloved ranch in California, the world didn't just lose a star. It lost a light. A guide. An example of how to live with joy, to age with grace, to love without condition, and to face even death with open arms.

Fans gathered. Flowers were laid. Songs played softly on radio stations and in homes around the world. And as tributes poured in from celebrities, politicians, co-stars, and everyday people whose lives she'd touched, a clear message emerged: Olivia was more than her roles. More than her records. She was, quite simply, *beloved.*

She left behind music. Memories. A legacy of healing. But most of all, she left behind a feeling – a kind of inner sunshine that makes you believe, if only for a moment, that maybe, just maybe... we *are* magic.

Because Olivia Newton-John didn't just believe in it. She *was* it.

19

Warm and Tender

"*Let me wrap you in my warm and tender love...*" - from *Warm and Tender* (1989)

There's a quiet kind of power in beginnings. Not the flashy kind, not the stadium-light moment of impact - but the seed, the soft spark, the first breath before the crescendo. That's what *If Not For You* was. Olivia Newton-John's debut solo album didn't launch with fireworks or fevered headlines. It crept in like dawn - warm, unsure, luminous. And yet, looking back now, it holds everything: the gentleness, the clarity, the deep sense of yearning wrapped in a voice so clean it sounded like hope itself.

"If not for you..." It's a line that loops back on itself when you're a fan. Because for so many of us, *if not for her*, things would've been different. Not necessarily dramatic things - not love won or lost or lives turned upside down - but *inner things*. The soundtrack to car rides with our mums. The album that got us through chemo. The movie we watched on repeat when we didn't feel seen. The song we slow danced to in socks on the kitchen floor. The cassette that taught us gentleness could be powerful. The voice that reminded us we didn't need to be loud to be loved.

By the time Olivia reached the final years of her career, she knew exactly who her music was for. Not for critics. Not for charts. Not for fashion. But for us. For the people who had walked with her since the early '70s and the children of those people who stumbled upon *Hopelessly Devoted to You* during a Grease rewatch and stayed for *Gaia*. For the quiet hearts. The dreamers. The hopefuls. The ones still searching for a light.

Olivia gave endlessly, and never once in a way that felt like performance. She wasn't playing a part. Not anymore. She was *offering*. Every concert in her later years felt like a gathering – a mutual remembering. Fans didn't just come to see her. They came to be with her. There was something sacred in that. Not worship. Not idolatry. Just love. Love passed back and forth like a candle from one set of hands to another.

And Olivia *always* made space for the fans. Long before social media turned every celebrity into a brand, she knew the power of real connection. She answered letters. She listened. She stayed after shows. She laughed with people who had waited hours just to say thank you. She never saw herself as separate. She was famous – yes – but she never stood above. Her grace was grounded.

It's fitting, then, that her legacy now rests not just in gold records or glittering awards – though she earned her share – but in the ripples. The cancer survivor who found strength in her interviews. The teenage girl who came out after watching Sandy's transformation and realised she could be soft *and* strong. The thousands who visit her wellness centre in Melbourne, seeking the kind of whole-person care Olivia once wished she'd had. The families who still gather for Sunday night *Grease* marathons, singing along to "Summer Nights" like it was written yesterday.

And what about *us* - the fans who can still remember the first time we heard her voice and felt something lift inside? We carry her too. Not just in playlists or signed albums or T-shirts folded carefully in drawers. But in how we treat people. How we move through the world. How we smile with warmth. How we offer softness in a world that too often prizes the sharp.

Because Olivia taught us that softness is not weakness. That peace is not passivity. That love, when offered without agenda, is the most radical thing a person can give.

She never needed to chase controversy. She never reinvented herself with shock. She didn't scream or demand. She simply *was*. And in being - in singing, in healing, in listening - she left the kind of mark no scandal, no gossip, no glitter bomb could ever replicate.

It's easy to forget, in the rush of celebrity and spectacle, how rare that is. But Olivia Newton-John never forgot who she was. From that first Bob Dylan cover in 1971 to her final duets with Chloe, she remained true to her tone - in voice and in spirit.

And for those of us who grew up with her, or found her late, or rediscovered her in grief or joy - the truth is simple: *If not for you*, Olivia, we'd be a little colder. A little less kind. A little less lit from within.

Thank you for giving us music. For giving us medicine. For

giving us moments.

Thank you for giving us *you*.

20

Carry Me Home

"*I can see the road beneath my feet so clearly now, like it was only yesterday...*" - from *Carry Me Home* (2006)

The last chapters of a life like Olivia Newton-John's don't arrive with fanfare or final bows. They arrive quietly - like waves returning to the shore, like a song that doesn't end, but fades into something softer. In the years that followed her final major tours and albums, Olivia didn't retreat. She *rooted*. Into family, into healing, into advocacy, into the kind of peace that only someone who has given the world everything can afford to hold.

She was never one for drama. Even when faced with one of life's fiercest adversaries - cancer - Olivia carried herself with a gentleness that was never mistaken for weakness. She didn't rage. She radiated. She met illness not as a foe to be battled in public headlines, but as a teacher, a path, a reality that needed compassion and change. Her cancer journey, which began in 1992 and recurred in later decades, wasn't just personal. It became a mission. And in true Olivia fashion, that mission took shape not with grim resolve, but with open arms.

The Olivia Newton-John Cancer Wellness & Research Centre in Melbourne wasn't a vanity project. It was a haven. A space rooted in her belief that healing isn't just about medicine - it's about music, light, nature, kindness. It's about being treated as a whole person, not a diagnosis. Olivia wanted people to walk into that place and feel seen, not as patients, but as precious lives worthy of gentleness. And they did.

Meanwhile, her own life took on a smaller rhythm - but never a lesser one. She spent time with her beloved husband John Easterling, whose herbal wisdom and unwavering support became a balm not only to her health but to her heart. She continued recording, sometimes in whispers - a spiritual album here, a healing track there. She collaborated with her daughter Chloe on songs that felt less like performances and more like shared prayers. Their voices twined together like branches, soft and certain.

And still, Olivia smiled. Still, she gave. Still, she showed up. Benefit concerts, breast cancer awareness campaigns, wellness retreats - she remained, until the very end, a woman of purpose. Her interviews in her later years were touched with the wisdom of someone who had made peace with life's impermanence but not with its preciousness. She didn't fear death. She feared not loving enough. Not giving enough. Not *being* enough for the people who still needed her warmth.

But of course, she *had* been. For decades. For lifetimes, it sometimes felt. Olivia had become something more than an entertainer. She was a thread through people's lives. A gentle constant. A reminder that kindness could be luminous, that vulnerability was strength, that one could live in the light even when the world grew dark.

When she passed away on August 8, 2022, the grief felt global, yet strangely intimate. It wasn't the kind of grief that explodes. It was the kind that settles in the chest, like a hush. Like someone dimming a lamp in a room you loved. Tributes poured in - from Elton, from Paul McCartney, from Dolly, from Grease co-stars and radio DJs, from fans who'd danced at their weddings to "Hopelessly Devoted to You" and parents who'd named their daughters Olivia in her honour. The outpouring wasn't just for a celebrity. It was for a companion. A light. A presence.

John Travolta's message was perhaps the most emblematic. "Yours from the moment I saw you and forever!" he wrote. It wasn't a line from a film. It was a love letter from one gentle soul to another. It reminded us that some connections - even when rooted in artifice - are utterly, achingly real.

And the music didn't stop. *Gaia* saw renewed interest. Fans clutched old vinyls with reverence. Young listeners discovered her for the first time - drawn in by TikToks and tribute videos and then staying for the albums that pulsed with truth. New voices covered "Magic" and "Xanadu." Grease was rewatched, and rewatched again. Suddenly, her legacy was not just nostalgia. It was *now*.

In the final recordings she made, Olivia's voice sounds quieter, yes, but clearer too - as if she were singing from just over the hill, the sound softened by distance but carried by love. She wasn't reaching for stardom anymore. She was reaching *through*. To hearts. To healing. To that place inside all of us that still believes in kindness as a radical act.

Her final chapter wasn't about saying goodbye. It was about being held. By her family. By her fans. By the millions of people she'd never met, but who carried her voice through surgeries, divorces, births, long car rides, lonely nights. And in return, Olivia allowed herself to be carried too - by grace, by memory, by the unshakable truth that she had mattered.

Because *she did.* She still does.

Olivia Newton-John's legacy is not a high note hit in 1978. It's not a glittering costume or a record deal. It's not even just the music - though the music will forever be part of her echo. Her legacy is the warmth. The steadiness. The quiet power of a woman who moved through decades of fame without ever losing sight of kindness.

She was, and is, a light. And while that light may now shine from somewhere beyond our sight, it hasn't dimmed. It's just moved. Shifted. Softened. Become something we carry - in our playlists, in our hearts, in how we speak to one another on the days we feel small.

Carry her home? No - she carried *us.* And we'll carry *her* for as long as her songs are sung, her stories are told, and her spirit is remembered with warmth and tenderness.

21

Hopelessly Devoted

"*My head is saying, 'Fool, forget him' / My heart is saying, 'Don't let go.'*" - from *Hopelessly Devoted to You* (1978)

There are love songs. And then there are Olivia Newton-John love songs. The kind that don't just echo through radio waves, but live in the fabric of our own stories. When Olivia stood in that hazy, pastel-lit garden in *Grease*, clutching a letter to Danny Zuko and singing of hopeless devotion, she wasn't just giving Sandy her solo - she was, in many ways, giving us all ours. It was a declaration not just of love, but of commitment. Tender, unwavering, and brave. The kind of commitment we, her fans, have felt ever since.

Because that's what Olivia inspired. Not just admiration. Not just nostalgia. But *devotion*. The kind that doesn't fade with time or fashion. The kind that holds firm when the spotlight dims and the chart positions stop mattering. The kind that lives quietly in the hearts of those who knew - truly knew - what it felt like to be seen, comforted, and carried by her voice.

To be devoted to Olivia Newton-John is not to be stuck in the past. It's to walk through life with a certain softness, a kind of gentle strength. To hum *Magic* while planting spring flowers. To play *Have You Never Been Mellow* while watching the rain streak down a train window. To hold *I Honestly Love You* close in the stillness after a funeral, or a wedding, or a moment of simply remembering that love - real love - leaves marks we're lucky to bear.

Her voice was velvet, yes, but also steel wrapped in satin. Olivia didn't belt. She *becalmed*. There was always a still centre in her delivery - a kind of grace that made the room quieter, the breath slower. Even at her most pop-perfect, she never shouted to be heard. She didn't have to. The world leaned in.

That's why, when her illness returned, we didn't just watch from afar. We followed. We rallied. We mourned and hoped and fundraised and prayed and played old records and bought new ones. Because when someone has given you decades of steadiness, of joy, of unwavering light - you give it back, in whatever ways you can. That's devotion. And it's never hopeless. It's holy.

In her final years, Olivia became something larger than a celebrity and more intimate than an icon. She was *familiar*. That cousin who always hugged you a little longer. That teacher whose praise still echoes years later. That voice you heard before you knew what falling in love felt like, and again when it fell apart. She was ours. And we were hers.

The Olivia Newton-John Cancer Wellness & Research Centre wasn't just a legacy project. It was a culmination. A place where science and spirit meet. A hospital with sunlight and music. A sanctuary built from everything she believed in: the power of healing, the importance of compassion, the necessity of touch and tenderness. She didn't just want to cure people. She wanted them to be *held*. And in that desire, she revealed the depth of her own faith – in life, in energy, in the soul's quiet journey.

And yet, she never made herself the centre of it. Olivia wasn't a martyr, and she never played the saint. She laughed often. She talked about cannabis and crystals and homegrown remedies with joy, not dogma. She aged with ease, not apology. She didn't resist change – she flowed with it. And in doing so, she modelled something quietly radical: that one can be graceful *and* gutsy. That strength can come wrapped in pastels and prayer beads.

Through every phase – the country ingénue, the pop queen, the activist, the mother, the healer – Olivia remained recognisable. Not just in face or voice, but in *energy*. You could feel it through the screen. You still can. Kindness isn't always visible, but with her, it radiated. She didn't have to tell you who she was. You *knew*.

And so, we stayed devoted. Through reinventions and returns. Through Gaia and Xanadu. Through duets with John Farnham and lullabies with Chloe. We didn't follow her because she was famous. We followed her because she made us feel *safe*. As if, no matter what was happening in our lives – grief, heartbreak, joy, uncertainty – there was someone out there singing just for us. Not to fix anything, but to remind us that we weren't alone.

In truth, her passing wasn't a moment of silence. It was a soft crescendo. A world lit with candles, tributes, playlists looping in bedrooms and kitchens and radios across the globe. It was John Travolta's trembling message. It was the Grease sing-alongs and the tears of grown men at the mention of her name. It was knowing, without doubt, that someone who had never met you could still have changed something in you. Forever.

Even now, it's hard to write about her in the past tense. Olivia Newton-John doesn't *feel* like the past. She feels like the breath before a note. The light just before sunset. The chorus you already know by heart. She feels *present* - not in body, but in essence. Because voices like hers don't vanish. They settle. In hearts. In homes. In the hush after a long day.

She never asked us for devotion. But we gave it freely. And she returned it a thousand times over. With every encore. Every gentle word. Every time she reached into her catalogue to give us not what was trendy, but what was true.

So what do we do with that now? We keep singing. We play her songs loud when we need joy, and soft when we need comfort. We tell younger generations not just who she was, but *how* she was. We wear our hopeless devotion like a badge of honour - not because we're stuck in the past, but because we believe, like she did, in the enduring beauty of love.

In the end, it wasn't hopeless at all. It was everything.

22

Author's Note: Thank You for Devoting With Me

From Bobby Gallagher

If you've made it this far, you already know: Olivia Newton-John was more than a singer. More than a Sandy. More than a chart-topper, cancer warrior, or style icon. She was *light* - poured into song. A steady hand for uncertain hearts. A beam of hope in a fickle world. And above all, she was *real*. Open-hearted. Graceful. Brave in soft ways. Her voice is the soundtrack to first kisses, lost summers, and long drives that saved us.

Writing this book hasn't been just a project - it's been a love letter. One I've wanted to write since I first heard *Hopelessly Devoted to You* on my mum's record player, wide-eyed and already a goner. And now, having travelled through every phase of her career – from country sweetness to pop perfection, from Grease lightning to Gaia earth-mother – I feel more devoted than ever.

To those who've cried reading these pages, danced in your kitchen to *Physical*, or simply remembered why Olivia mattered – thank you. We're part of something beautiful. We are the fans who never let go. Hopelessly? Yes. But also joyfully. Eternally.

Here's to ONJ. And here's to us.

Bobby

23

Discography: Olivia Newton-John

Studio Albums

1. *If Not for You* (1971)
2. *Olivia* (1972)
3. *Let Me Be There* (1973)
4. *Long Live Love* (1974)
5. *Have You Never Been Mellow* (1975)
6. *Clearly Love* (1975)
7. *Come On Over* (1976)
8. *Don't Stop Believin'* (1976)
9. *Making a Good Thing Better* (1977)
10. *Totally Hot* (1978)
11. *Physical* (1981)
12. *Soul Kiss* (1985)
13. *The Rumour* (1988)
14. *Warm and Tender* (1989)
15. *Gaia: One Woman's Journey* (1994)
16. *Back with a Heart* (1998)

17. *(2)* (2002) – duets album
18. *Indigo: Women of Song* (2004)
19. *Grace and Gratitude* (2006)
20. *Christmas Wish* (2007)
21. *A Celebration in Song* (2008) – duets
22. *Liv On* (2016) – with Amy Sky & Beth Nielsen Chapman
23. *Friends for Christmas* (2016) – with John Farnham

Soundtracks

- *Grease* (1978) – with John Travolta
- *Xanadu* (1980) – with Electric Light Orchestra
- *A Few Best Men: Original Soundtrack* (2012)

Live Albums

- *Love Performance* (1981, Japan-only)
- *Live in Japan* (2010)
- *Summer Nights: Live in Las Vegas* (2015)

Key Compilation Albums

- *Greatest Hits* (1977)
- *Greatest Hits Vol. 2* (1982)
- *Back to Basics: The Essential Collection 1971–1992* (1992)
- *Gold* (2005)
- *40/40: The Best Selection* (2010, Japan)
- *Hopelessly Devoted: The Hits* (2022)

Notable Singles (Selected Highlights)

- *If Not for You* (1971)
- *Let Me Be There* (1973)
- *I Honestly Love You* (1974)
- *Have You Never Been Mellow* (1975)
- *Please Mr. Please* (1975)
- *Don't Stop Believin'* (1976)
- *Hopelessly Devoted to You* (1978)
- *You're the One That I Want* (1978) – duet with John Travolta
- *Summer Nights* (1978) – duet with John Travolta
- *A Little More Love* (1978)
- *Deeper Than the Night* (1979)
- *Magic* (1980)
- *Xanadu* (1980) – with ELO
- *Physical* (1981)
- *Make a Move on Me* (1982)
- *Heart Attack* (1982)
- *Twist of Fate* (1983)
- *Soul Kiss* (1985)
- *The Rumour* (1988)
- *Not Gonna Give In to It* (1994)
- *Love Is a Gift* (1998)
- *Let's Get Physical 2021* – remix with Dua Lipa (posthumous fan tribute mix)

24

Fan Fun

☆ The Hopelessly Devoted Fan Quiz ☆

A 20-question Olivia Newton-John trivia challenge for true blue fans

Test your knowledge, relive the magic, and see just how "Physical" your fandom
   really is! Scroll slowly - answers are at the end!

1. What was Olivia's first solo single to chart in the U.S.?

A) Please Mr. Please
   B) If Not for You
   C) Banks of the Ohio
   D) Let Me Be There

2. Which superstar produced Olivia's 1971 debut album?

A) Barry Gibb
   B) Elton John
   C) Bruce Welch
   D) Jeff Lynne

3. What song did Olivia win her first Grammy for?

A) I Honestly Love You
   B) Physical
   C) Have You Never Been Mellow
   D) Magic

4. What musical film features the duet "You're the One That I Want"?

A) Xanadu
   B) Grease
   C) Saturday Night Fever
   D) Moulin Rouge

5. Olivia represented the UK in which international competition?

A) Eurovision Song Contest
   B) American Idol
   C) Sanremo Music Festival
   D) The Voice UK

6. What was the name of her character in Grease?

A) Sandy Anderson
   B) Cindy Lawson
   C) Sandy Olsson
   D) Olivia Sanders

7. Which ELO-fronted soundtrack featured Olivia singing the title track?

A) Discovery
   B) Time
   C) Xanadu
   D) Eldorado

8. Which single spent 10 weeks at No. 1 on the U.S. Billboard Hot 100?

A) Magic
   B) Physical
   C) Twist of Fate
   D) Summer Nights

9. What is the name of Olivia's only child?

A) Bella
   B) Chloe
   C) Sophie
   D) Grace

10. Olivia starred opposite which actor in Two of a Kind (1983)?

A) Patrick Swayze
   B) Richard Gere
   C) John Travolta
   D) Michael Douglas

11. What was the name of Olivia's environmental-themed album from 1994?

A) Gaia: One Woman's Journey
   B) Natural Woman
   C) Earth Calling
   D) Back to Nature

12. What hit song begins with the lyric, "Guess mine is not the first heart broken"?

A) Please Mr. Please
   B) Twist of Fate
   C) Hopelessly Devoted to You
   D) Deeper Than the Night

13. Olivia was born in which country?

A) Australia
   B) England
   C) New Zealand
   D) The United States

14. What iconic workout-themed single became her biggest global hit?

A) Let's Get Physical
   B) Physical
   C) Fit
   D) Stronger

15. What was Olivia's final studio album of original material (not a duet or Christmas album)?

A) Indigo
   B) Grace and Gratitude
   C) Liv On
   D) Gaia

16. Olivia co-founded what kind of wellness facility in Melbourne?

A) Yoga studio
   B) Spa retreat
   C) Cancer wellness & research centre
   D) Animal therapy clinic

17. Which duet partner appeared with her on "Suddenly"?

A) Cliff Richard
   B) John Travolta
   C) Barry Gibb
   D) Cliff Richard

18. What was Olivia's profession before she became a global pop star?

A) Kindergarten teacher
   B) Hairdresser
   C) Pet store clerk
   D) Singer in a coffee house band

19. Olivia Newton-John played Kira in which movie?

A) Grease
   B) Xanadu
   C) Gaia
   D) Two of a Kind

20. In what year did Olivia Newton-John pass away?

A) 2020
  B) 2021
  C) 2022
  D) 2023

✓ Answers

1. B) If Not for You
2. C) Bruce Welch
3. A) I Honestly Love You
4. B) Grease
5. A) Eurovision Song Contest
6. C) Sandy Olsson
7. C) Xanadu
8. B) Physical
9. B) Chloe
10. C) John Travolta
11. A) Gaia: One Woman's Journey
12. C) Hopelessly Devoted to You
13. B) England
14. B) Physical
15. B) Grace and Gratitude
16. C) Cancer wellness & research centre
17. D) Cliff Richard
18. D) Singer in a coffee house band
19. B) Xanadu
20. C) 2022

🎤 Score yourself, pop star!

18–20 correct – You're *Totally Hot* – Livvy lives in your soul.

14–17 correct – You're *Magic* – your knowledge glows like neon roller disco.

10–13 correct – *Have You Never Been Mellow?* Maybe time for a rewatch of *Grease*.

0–9 correct – Don't worry… you're still "The One That We Want." Play the records. Start again.

Printed in Dunstable, United Kingdom